"In this insightful and inspiring book, Frank Joseph explores the many dimensions of meaningful coincidences—synchronicities—events that all of us have experienced at some time in our lives . . . *Synchronicity & You* is a valuable guide book that not only informs but also leads us, step by step, into communication with our deeper subconscious nature and nudges open the gate to our inner self—to the domain of synchronicity."

From the Foreword by Dale Graff,
Author, *Tracks in the Psychic Wilderness*

"In *Synchronicity & You*, Frank Joseph takes us beyond the sensational stories and the scientific debates into the very heart and soul of synchronicity. This is a masterpiece of a book written with the profound insight, clarity, and awe that can only come from first-hand personal experience. Joseph weaves together hundreds of striking synchronicity examples along a series of major recognizable themes selected to astonish, fascinate, move, and amuse us. A first-class book for anyone who wants to widen horizons and deepen self-discovery!"

Suzanne V. Brown, Ph.D.
Editor, *The Synchronicity Connection*

"Frank Joseph has written a fascinating and well-researched look at the multi-faceted role that synchronicity plays in our lives. He explores not only the philosophical implications of meaningful coincidence, but also offers practical suggestions and tips for readers to recognize synchronicity in their own lives—thus opening the door to a better understanding of themselves and the universe we all inhabit."

Ray Grasse
Author, *The Waking Dream: Unlocking the Symbolic Language of Our Lives*

Synchronicity & You

Frank Joseph

ELEMENT

Boston, Massachusetts • Shaftesbury, Dorset
Melbourne, Victoria

© Element Books, Inc. 1999
Text © Frank Joseph 1999

First published in the USA in 1999 by
Element Books, Inc.
160 North Washington Street
Boston, Massachusetts 02114

Published in Great Britain in 1999 by
Element Books Limited
Shaftesbury, Dorset SP7 8BP

Published in Australia in 1999 by
Element Books Limited for
Penguin Books Australia Limited
487 Maroondah Highway, Ringwood, Victoria 3134

Library of Congress Cataloging-in-Publication data available

British Library Cataloguing in Publication data available

First Edition
10 9 8 7 6 5 4 3 2 1

Printed and bound in the United States by Courier

ISBN 1-86204-383-3

To my father, Max.

Contents

Foreword

In this insightful and inspiring book, Frank Joseph explores the many dimensions of meaningful coincidences—synchronicities; events that all of us have experienced at some time in our lives, whether we consciously recognize them or not. Frank Joseph presents a broad perspective of synchronistic phenomenon while also retaining individual and personal examples—those down to earth incidents that ring loudly the reality of this "helping hand" and that illustrate how readily available synchronicity can be for anyone.

Synchronistic assistance, whether in response to a clear need or for reasons beyond our conscious awareness, can range from apparent minor incidents to those that have a profound impact on our lives including those that are life transforming or even life saving. Through his own explorations, Frank Joseph has discovered that synchronistic events occur more frequently than we usually realize—an observation not recognized by other books on synchronicity. He is absolutely correct! *Synchronicity & You*, therefore, can have a transforming effect on us; it invites—even challenges—us to be open to our own synchronistic nature. It offers sound practical advice on how to become more alert to synchronicities and how to increase their occurrence.

It should come as no surprise that the key to tapping into the domain of synchronicity is the keeping of a dedicated journal. Journal writing allows us to record synchronistic events for later review and inspiration. Through the act of writing, we send a signal to our subconscious processes that reinforces our interest and desire for new synchronicities.

I can affirm from my own experiences the value of journal keeping. In 1970, after a startling synchronistic event, I started a dream diary. This quickly expanded into a journal with a variety of information—key daily activity, dreams, intuitions, psychic occurrences and synchronicities. The journal also gave me an excuse to begin writing. Little did I realize it then, but decades later this journal would become the lodestone for new creative activities and the beginning of a writing/lecturing career.

I know that anyone who decides to actually begin journal keeping will eventually discover its value. Journal keeping is a co-creative process; it is a way for you to discover or uncover previously unknown aspects and capabilities of yourself. It is a great way to engage in an active process of inner growth and expanded self-awareness.

As a framework for understanding synchronicity, Frank Joseph presents a broad historical perspective of how synchronicity events have been experienced, or manifested, over the centuries and for various cultures. We are certainly not experiencing a new phenomenon, but are in fact reconnecting with the very essence of primordial life itself and to the roots of timeless consciousness. Through synchronicities, we are in direct touch with our elemental ground state of being. Synchronicities point toward an organizational principle of the universe and suggest that our connection with a higher order of consciousness is never far from the surface of ordinary awareness. In one sense, synchronicity can be seen as a meaningful intersection of paths; and in another, as an interface or interpenetrating with an alternative dimension of reality.

The idea of synchronicity has a counterpart in quantum physics. Recent experiments show that certain paired elementary particles retain instantaneous knowledge of changes made to one of the pairs, even when they are separated at great distances. This phenomenon—a "nonlocal" effect—is acausal. That is, it has no known mechanism that can explain its occurrence. The elementary basis of quantum mechanics is also acausal. Synchronicities are an acausal "connecting principle" between people or events.

Thus, the fundamental aspects of the physical and mental modes of reality have a similar ground of being. The purpose seems to be for remaining connected and for communicating information. At a personal level, then, synchronistic experiences can also serve as a pathway, as a bridge for communication, with others and with the creative source of our universe.

But how can we be sure we have in fact encountered a synchronicity? How do we separate synchronicity from mere chance? Certainly, the correlation of need and timing are guideposts, especially when the event is beyond rationalization or statistical logic. Here the author gives us keen insight: Examine your own feelings. Did the experience invoke a sense of awe or mystery? Did the experience stir up, through some type of deep resonance, a feeling of truth, an intuitive knowing? Did we feel less alone, as if touched by a mysterious and hidden co-creative partner? Did the experience generate high motivation and energy, even passion, for a new activity drawing on potentials not previously suspected? Certainly, such experiences can bring greater confidence into our lives and can empower us. We now have a new purpose and meaning for our life. We develop or enhance our creativity—or co-creativity—for serving all life and feel a compassion for all living things and our environment.

Synchronicities, in the author's view, can be seen as "little miracles" through which an otherwise unseen but non-forceful consciousness manifests itself into our lives. Free will is retained, however. We always have the choice, as many people select, to ignore, even ridicule, this inner partner, our inner source of synchronistic help. But that is their choice. Clearly, it need not be ours.

There are patterns in synchronicities, like on an artful mosaic. By being open to them, we soon discover our unique role within the larger designs of life and evolution. We can become an active part of the whole, and in a holistic way, co-creators in a participatory universe. A thorough reading of *Synchronicity & You* will help us begin a fascinating new creative journey of discovery, and bring us into contact with our synchronistic nature.

Synchronicity & You is a valuable guide book that not only informs but also leads us, step by step, into communication with our deeper subconscious nature and nudges open the gate to our inner self—to the domain of synchronicity.

Dale Graff
Author, Tracks in the Psychic Wilderness

Introduction

What Is Synchronicity?

The Secret of the world is the tie between person and event.

—Ralph Waldo Emerson, *Fate*

The term *synchronicity* was coined by one of the twentieth century's most influential thinkers, the Swiss psychologist Carl Gustav Jung. He defined synchronicity as any apparent coincidence that inspires a sense of wonder and personal meaning or particular significance in the observer. It is a perceived connection between two or more objects, events, or persons without any recognizable cause. He used the term for the first time in 1930 to describe a situation in which apparently unrelated events converge to form a shared experience regarded as momentous by the person or persons experiencing it.

An example of synchronicity is when, for no apparent reason, you suddenly remember a friend you have not thought of or heard from in years, and just then the telephone rings and the voice on the other end belongs to the recollected person. Did you experience mental telepathy, or was it something else, something even more inexplicable?

Or perhaps you must be on time for a critically important appointment. It is one of the turning points of your career. However, the location for your pivotal meeting is downtown in a crowded city, and nearby parking is nowhere to be found. Traffic is heavy with other motorists also in search of a space. But just as you arrive before the very building where you are expected, a car pulls out in front of you, leaving an empty spot a few paces from the main entrance. How could such a fortuitous set of circumstances have come about?

You might be faced with a large, unpaid bill that threatens all kinds of havoc in your life. You have exhausted every possible means of paying it off. On the very day the axe is supposed to fall, you receive a tax refund larger than expected. It is precisely the amount of money owed. What were the odds against the tax refund not only exactly corresponding to the debt but arriving at the last moment?

These are typical instances of synchronicity, or meaningful coincidence; events like these happen to millions of people every day. They are common enough, and most people who experience them, after initial feelings of strangeness, forget about them or dismiss them as inevitable but trifling quirks of life classified under luck, good or bad. But "luck" is no explanation and suggests the random aimlessness of fortune. A closer examination of such phenomena suggests there is much more to them. While individual instances of synchronicity may seem trivial, they assume startling magnitudes of influence when seen in the bigger picture of their role in our lives. Synchronicity is a connection linking the individual to whom the event occurs with a nonmaterial reality beyond our physical plane. This otherwise invisible reality is the organizing power underlying and interpenetrating all things in the universe, a power some refer to as "God," "Fate," "Evolution," or by any number of other names.

Synchronicities are those instances when two dimensions momentarily interface, with the receiving individual acting as the contact point. Such an Otherworld can no longer be shelved as purely theoretical. Proof of its parallel existence is offered in harder evidence than that of all the philosophies and religions that have suspected or affirmed it for thousands of years, or the latest research in subatomic physics, which is in the process of documenting it. Hundreds of books, old and new, treat the subject from the perspectives of these broad, often esoteric, intellectual disciplines.

But meaningful coincidences do not confine themselves to the experiences of philosophers, theologians, or scientists. Meaningful coincidences happen to everyone, regardless of intellectual background. They are similar to the lightning that connects heaven and earth in a brief, dramatic moment. And the person to whom they occur is by far best qualified to comprehend them, if only because they appear to be personal gifts from a great, caring intelligence responsible for the destiny of the universe.

Synchronicity & You is a practical handbook. It offers a direct means to define the significant coincidences we encounter and provides a simple method for decoding them. Not content with unsupported statements of opinion, *Synchronicity & You* uses straightforward language to demonstrate how this otherwise inexplicable phenomenon operates, and, more important, how to make it work for you. Major categories of synchronous events are listed and illustrated with examples, followed by a simple, universally applicable technique to successfully access the meaning of synchronicities you might encounter.

Crystallizing the insights of ancient myth, *Synchronicity & You* finally provides a clear, credible explanation of synchronicity's origins, function, and importance for every person's well-being, spiritual life, and destiny. The full appreciation of synchronicity establishes a deepened sense of identity and self-worth, while giving meaning, direction, and purpose to our existence. In its highest manifestations, synchronicity is nothing less than our personal connection with the Ultimate Mystery of the universe.

My chief purpose in writing *Synchronicity & You* has been to explain this common though personally significant mystery and offer ways for everyday readers to actually put it to use as an important adjunct to their lives. I became interested in the enigma through an experience described in chapter 1. I was less inspired to write about it than to understand it. Virtually all the books I could find on the subject offered brilliant insights into the phenomenon, but none of them could explain it, except in the most theoretical terms. I sought answers among my friends, and they shared with me anecdotes about the sometimes poignant, occasionally humorous coincidences they had experienced. It was particularly surprising to learn that some individuals encountered moments of high synchronicity that were the most important episodes of their lives, strange incidents that quite literally transformed them. Intrigued by such personal testimony, I never missed an opportunity over the next several years to question virtually anyone with whom I came into contact. Almost without exception, people were enthusiastic in describing their own tales of meaningful coincidence.

It was during these informal interviews that certain recurring patterns began to emerge. Clearly, there was not only a commonality of experience, but there were common themes that surfaced in the reports of individuals absolutely unknown to one another. I was astonished to observe that some of the patterns observed in others were evidenced in my own synchronicities, which I began to record in a journal specifically for that purpose. I found this journal to be an important tool that merits its own chapter (chapter 9).

Learning that synchronous events led to profound self-discoveries in those who experienced them and feeling certain that these events were experienced by most, if not all, of my fellow humans, prompted me to share with others what I was able to learn from the one hundred persons I interviewed. I also wanted others to learn and use the simple, directly effective methods I had developed to understand the synchronicities we encounter. Although the subject practically obsessed me with its compelling enigmas, it was like nothing else I had ever attempted to describe. Most of my published books and magazine articles dealt with aviation and ancient history, while my background as the editor-in-chief of a national archaeology periodical, *Ancient American*, had little to do with parapsychology. Only my several books about sacred sites and a class on the same subject I taught at the Open University of Minnesota occasionally touched on the potential for meaningful coincidences found in the world's strangely hallowed locations. However, training at Southern Illinois University's School of Journalism and experience as an investigative reporter for Chicago's *Winnetka Paper* did equip me for getting to the bottom of a story and writing it up in clear language most readers could easily grasp. And synchronicity seemed to me a hot story worth investigating.

Whatever reluctance I might have felt in presenting my manuscript to the public was dispelled by Ralph Scott, Ph.D., head of the Department of Educational Psychology at the University of Northern Iowa in Cedar Falls, and an officer of the American Board of Professional Psychology. His kind words for *Synchronicity & You* and plans to include it as a teaching aide in his psychology classes gave me the self-assurance to go public with my work. Thanks to Dr. Scott and the friends who lent themselves to my research group, I feel confident in promising my readers this: *Synchronicity & You* will help you understand the purpose of meaningful coincidence in your life.

chapter 1

The Magic of Meaningful Coincidence

There is an endless net of threads throughout the universe. The horizontal threads are in space. The vertical threads are in time. At every crossing of the threads, there is an individual. And every individual is a crystal bead. The great light of an Absolute Being illuminates and penetrates every crystal bead. And every crystal bead reflects not only the light from every other crystal in the net, but also every other reflection throughout the entire universe.

—The *Rig Veda*

Even though the words of the *Rig Veda* were written more than 3,500 years ago, the concept they describe strikes us as unexpectedly up-to-date, considering the vast gulf of years separating our time from the composition of this greatest literary achievement of ancient India. It surprises us that the unknown author of this insightful epic living so long before the advent of science could have been capable of making such a modern deduction. On a personal level, this passage seems to tell us something we have long known or suspected but perhaps never deliberately expressed or put into words, and certainly never stated so poetically. It has a fundamental ring of truth echoing across thousands of years from a culture radically unlike our own. Otherwise these words would not have such a profound effect on us.

Referred to in the *Rig Veda* as "Indra's Net," its analogy of creation as a vast web of interrelated existences underscores synchronicity's chief implication: Namely, that the otherwise invisible, spiritual bonds connecting every detail of the universe suddenly appear where they intersect. As the Rig Veda puts it, when a crystal in Indra's net reflects on another crystal, the result is a perceptible, meaningful coincidence. Appropriately, Indra is the universal Vedic god, the Lord of Time, who catches all things in his cosmic net.

Emerson used the same analogy to connect Indra's Net with Jung's synchronicity in the following century.

> *Every particular in nature, a leaf, a drop, a crystal, a moment in time is related to the whole. So·intimate is this Unity, that, it is easily seen, it lies under the undermost garment of nature, and betrays its source in universal Spirit. For, it pervades Thought also.* (Emerson, p. 385)

Emerson, too, saw the vast interconnectedness of existence as a

> *web of relation. But to see how fate slides into freedom and freedom into fate, observe how far the roots of every creature run, or find if you can a point where there is no thread of connection. Our life is consentaneous and far-related. This knot of nature is so well tied that nobody was ever cunning enough to find the two ends.* (Emerson, p. 366)

A modern example of this unseen power serves to illustrate: On a late afternoon in the early spring of 1992, I was driving home from work on Interstate 57. Nothing about the circumstances of my brief, everyday trip to the south suburbs of Chicago was outstanding or unusual in any way. Although my thoughts were neither drifting nor preoccupied, I was peacefully alert, relaxed and enjoying the countryside, which was beginning to green up after the vernal equinox. The radio was off, and traffic was not heavy.

Only moments before I arrived at the east-west I-80 expressway, the words "Salman Rushdie" suddenly began running through my mind. Although the words produced no anxiety or emotions of any kind in me, they seemed to drift in from nowhere with a recurrent insistence I could not understand. I wondered why my mind had suddenly chosen to focus on the name of a famous person of whom I was only remotely aware and in whom I was even less interested. I knew vaguely that his novel had so aroused the indignation of Muslims around the world they had openly declared their intention to kill him. A heretical writer pursued by benighted religious fanatics—why would this pop into my mind?

Yet, here was his name persistently running through my mind for no reason. I did not recall hearing it recently on any news broadcasts, nor had I read about the fugitive author for many months. "Rushdie, Rushdie, Rushdie." The endless loop carrying his name through my brain went on for about one minute. Crossing over I-80, I deliberately willed the annoyance into oblivion.

I had just done so, when a dark blue Buick came up along the off-ramp on my right from the expressway below. Nothing about the vehicle seemed extraordinary, although it was speeding a bit—more typical than unusual for Illinois drivers. I hardly paid any attention to the car, except to allow it to enter my lane at a safe distance. But as it pulled in front of me, my eyes were drawn to the license plate, which read simply, in bold, capital letters, "RUSHDIE."

I laughed out loud in surprise. But almost at once a powerful, inexpressible sensation of awe and wonder washed over me. I was suddenly in the presence of some mystical force or personality. The Rushdie Buick continued down I-57, while I exited at the next off-ramp, my mind vigorously pondering the odds against such an occurrence. They seemed incalculable, representing a thing beyond probability. I thought back to all the events of the day. The slightest alteration of any one of them, by so much as a minute or less, would have made me miss my encounter. Moreover, the coincidence did not *feel* like a statistical inevitability, the mundane result of probability. I was convinced in my heart that the expressway coincidence was meaningful in some way.

Perhaps my subconscious picked up on the brain waves of the Rushdie-car driver, so much so that they broke through to my conscious mind with a name that made no sense at first. On the surface of it, a random telepathic link seemed to explain an occurrence that was not scientifically provable, because it could not be duplicated under laboratory conditions. Yet, it had actually existed in space and time. However, as I reexamined the incident, especially my own immediate reaction to it, a telepathic cause began to sit less comfortably as a final explanation, chiefly because I could not shake the feeling that the encounter was somehow deeply meaningful. I would have been delighted with a personal demonstration of mental telepathy. But, while it may have played a part in the encounter, telepathy was just that—a part of something else, something larger.

The man, Salman Rushdie, and his dilemma did not comprise The Meaning. He still meant nothing to me. I felt no compulsion to rush out and purchase his *Satanic Verses*. Maybe an answer lay not in the writer but in the name itself: *Rush die*, as in "rushing to die." The driver of the Rushdie car was speeding, after all, although a traffic accident did not seem likely at the moment. Could it have been that I was precognitively alerted to the speeder, thereby avoiding a dangerous situation? If this were true, then one would be inclined to conclude that some sympathetic intelligence that oversaw my human affairs intervened to subtly prevent a possibly lethal situation. In so doing, however, this intelligent benefactor had tipped his hand and demonstrated his existence when he showed me an acausal event in a universe run entirely and exclusively on cause and effect—or so we have come to believe.

But handy answers that such incidents are manifestations of God, angels, the devil, statistical probability, psychic abilities, and the rest explain nothing. Even my own best interpretation of the event seemed inadequate. A nagging, unaccountably meaningful enigma had entered my life, however fleetingly, and the mysterious awe of the experience continued to impress me. It was by no means the first of its kind I had encountered. I could remember a few others, but I had shelved them all as the inconsequential coincidences, the inevitable, random events, however well-timed they might be, that naturally attend human existence.

The Salman Rushdie incident cast an entirely different light on such occurrences, and I was determined to learn as much as I could about them. In my naive enthusiasm, I was like the young Parsifal, the Pure Fool, who confidently rides off to find the Holy Grail without the slightest notion of what it is or of the difficulties involved in obtaining it. I hardly knew where to begin. The very nature of synchronicity is fleeting and amorphous.

More problematic than even such fringe curiosities as UFOs, Big Foot, ghosts, or mermaids, synchronicity does not allow itself to be photographed or subjected to laboratory examination. It relies for its study entirely on personal testimony. Yet, it is encountered by so many people that its existence has always been generally acknowledged. Any discussion of meaningful coincidences must necessarily be subjective, because they are personally significant to the individuals who experience them.

Scientific objectivity, the means by which we determine truths about our material world, cannot get a grip on the phenomenon. So skeptics who insist that nothing is real outside the scientific process dismiss synchronous encounters as nonevents, the fantasies of contemporary superstition. Indeed, to even admit they exist at once throws down the gauntlet to our accepted perception of the universe as irrevocably governed by the basic principles of cause and effect in terms of definable space and linear time—a challenge of enormous implications.

My investigation over the next six years began in the usual way: I read everything I could find about the subject, starting with Jung's seminal work, *Synchronicity, an Acausal Connecting Principle*, pursing the ongoing studies of his followers, like Marie-Louise von Franz, and continuing with what researchers are currently offering, as well as the latest magazine articles in *Quest*, *Fate*, and *Psychology Today*. All these writers were physicists, psychologists, or parapsychologists. And while they certainly define and broaden our understanding of the phenomenon and provide a variety of working models from which to choose, their own disciplines or world views, which enable them to undertake their inquiries, also limit them and prevent them from reaching a final solution. They all stop short of these key questions: *What are the origins of synchronicity? If it is significant, why? What use is it? Can anything of value be derived from it? Most important, where does it come from? What does it mean?*

At best, these writers answered with intriguing speculations, which doubtless made for stimulating arguments among their multidegreed colleagues but left everyone else wondering what they were talking about. It was, however, enlightening to learn that the problem was not as modern as I'd assumed. Jung, while he invented the term, was by no means the first to investigate synchronicity, and he admitted his debt to the "Philosopher of Pessimism," Arthur Schopenhauer, who was amazed by the "Apparent Deliberateness in the Fate of the Individual" (the title of his groundbreaking essay on the subject) as far back as 1851. Nearly two hundred years earlier, another influential German thinker, Gottfried Wilhelm Leibniz, conceived "his idea of pre-established harmony, that is, an absolute synchronism of psychic and physical events" (Krassner, p. 114).

Surprisingly, as long ago as the Enlightenment, the Renaissance, and the Middle Ages, even back during classical civilization and before that in the Bronze Age, perhaps even in prehistory, meaningful coincidences preoccupied the minds of humans. Given that venerable pedigree, synchronicity could not be dismissed as a modern superstition, especially when it was so seriously investigated by many of the world's greatest thinkers, then and now. The problem still seems to be this: synchronicity is irrational and illogical, and it defies clinical examination.

Science, philosophy, and myth have laid a good foundation upon which to build hypotheses for understanding synchronicity in general terms through a number of plausible theories, but they have not constructed an edifice or even a framework to support the final answers. It is imperative that any investigator seeking the ultimate truth about synchronicity examine people who encounter meaningful coincidence, compare their experiences with those of others, and consider their own thoughts, reactions, and opinions. Such subjective experiences are far more important than the pronouncements of physics or psychology on these matters, just as the insights of a less-educated traveler who returns from a little-known land will be more valuable because of his personal experiences than those of the most brilliant scholar who has read about the same country but never been there.

Beginning in 1992, I interviewed one hundred people about their synchronous encounters. They were from all backgrounds and walks of life, ranging from children in grammar school to seniors in their nineties, from students and factory workers to airline pilots and university professors. More significant, they held a wide variety of beliefs. In addition to representatives of the major religious denominations, there were also New Agers, agnostics, atheists, pagans, Wiccans, Christian mystics, and, in many cases, people who never cared much or thought about spiritual or metaphysical matters of any kind. Yet, all of them, with only three exceptions, freely confessed that meaningful coincidences played major roles in their personal histories, often occurring at a major junction in their lives. One of the trio unimpressed with synchronicity included (most surprisingly) a professional psychologist, who defined it as an "epiphenomenon," or nothing more than random, insignificant happenings artificially assigned meaning by self-deceiving individuals. Another was an agnostic, who believed that "when you're dead, you're dead." The third was a cynic, who declared, "God is a sadist." Strangely enough, the same agnostic was a dedicated amateur botanist who marveled at the reproductive miracle of his plants. "I can't understand it," he often muttered in amazement, while admiring the complex internal organization of a simple seed.

These three people presented a sharp contrast to the other ninety-seven men, women, and children, a few of whom gave their lives over entirely to synchronicity, following implicitly and without question every meaningful coincidence that touched their day-to-day affairs. Although less engaged but more "rational" people might imagine that such blind faith in acausal events would instantly lead to chaos, I found that those who steered the course of their existence according to such mystical instructions possessed an extraordinarily strong sense of purpose in their lives. In several cases they described earlier years when they were "out of sync" with their environment and involved in self-destructive behavior, until some transformational coincidence changed their lives.

By following every synchronicity, they emerged from chaotic survival with a sense of balance, harmony, and inner quiet that had previously eluded them. They now go through life with a feeling of place. Although material abundance does not usually accompany them, they are typically busy with numerous projects that enrich their lives with personal fulfillment and excitement. They almost always preserve their acute mental faculties and an active sense of humor into extreme old age. This is not to suggest they do not have their fits of depression or suffer from all the afflictions attendant to their fellow human beings. They differ only in their superior abilities to cope under the aegis of some sympathetic guidance that manifests itself in meaningful coincidences. Far from plummeting into chaos, individuals who faithfully follow such guidance lead orderly, self-disciplined lives of which compassion and creativity are often the hallmarks.

Even more remarkable, their lives take on a truly magical quality; the right person, place, or thing is always entering their lives at strategic moments. An overdue telephone bill that threatens to disconnect service in the next twenty-four hours is inadvertently paid at the last conceivable moment by a client who happens to work for the phone company. While a writer is researching an obscure subject, experts in the field contact her for no particular reason with precisely the facts she needs, or books literally fall open to pages describing the desired information. These kinds of events can happen to anyone, but when you live your life by synchronicity, they occur constantly. It may be difficult at first to take the great leap of faith, nakedly entrusting your life to the unseen powers of the universe. But, contrary to what Dr. Jean Shinoda Bolen claims in her wonderfully insightful *The Tao of Psychology*, such people do not abdicate logical thought, nor do they feel dominated by omens (pp. 47, 48). Far from limiting the range of information available for processing and assessment, living by synchronicity enormously broadens informational horizons. "Synchronicity has never led me astray," one follower told me. According to a young woman who describes herself as an "intuitive artist," "The more you act on your feelings and take the risk of checking out the validity of your intuition, the more reliable it can become."

Even the most dedicated advocates of synchronicity are not so one-sided or myopically focused that their rational walk through the world has been impaired. Indeed, if we accept that meaningful coincidences are messages, instructions, advice, warnings, and guidance to us from our environment, from our inner selves where the ultimate truth of our identity sits, and/or from the organizing power of the universe, then we realize that the information given to us must be truthful and for our benefit. Consider the source. But be warned: to implicitly obey every synchronicity is to take the off-ramp from the common expressway of mundane existence for the hero's journey, the spiritual path only you can travel. The difficulties and dangers may be formidable, the riches of materialism less accessible. But you will be living the Authentic Life and led to higher and higher levels of your own personal truth.

The majority of the people I interviewed found the lofty paths offered by total dedication to synchronicity too challenging to embrace completely. They were content to live in the mundane world but wanted to enhance the quality, especially the spiritual quality, of their lives by accepting the most obvious meaningful coincidences as important guidance.

Clearly, the testimony of individuals willing to discuss synchronicity was far more instructive than all the scientific tomes on the subject put together. The experiences and reactions of those interviewed combined to build a sturdy framework of useful information needed to construct an explanation for the enigma. But while they provided a wonderful, truly organic overview of the phenomenon, they needed to be reinforced by a close-up view. The very nature of acausal events is, after all, personally subjective, and, while the experiences of others and the theories of profound thinkers provide the research structure's foundation and scaffolding, a thorough examination of synchronicity needs the center support of a single life, any life, examined in detail for its synchronicity.

I therefore vowed to straightforwardly record every meaningful coincidence I encountered, no matter how significant or insignificant, and to refrain from comment, embellishment, or judgment on each one. I faithfully maintained a dated synchronicity journal in company with another diary, in which I dispassionately wrote down every dream I had, no matter how imperfectly I remembered it. Wondering even then, at the outset of my research, if some dreams contained elements of synchronicity, I wanted to discover if a relationship between the two actually existed. Early confirmation of this suspicion soon justified my strict coordination of the dream diary with its companion synchronicity journal.

I documented every dream and acausal event, studied and noted the findings of experts, and investigated the meaningful coincidences of others. After five years of work, the time had come to make sense, if possible, of all the collected material. For the first time, I examined both records of my dreams and synchronicities in their entirety. What opened before me was more than I expected to find. It was astonishing to observe the recurring themes and discernable patterns that interfaced unconscious sleep with waking reality. I could scarcely believe my own handwriting. It was like reading the script of a theatrical play in which a character was given cues for stage action by some unseen director. Only then did it occur to me how incredibly magical my life had been over the past several years. It is so easy to forget the numerous synchronicities that happen to us. But here, all were documented, their finely woven interrelationships and the major roles they combined to play in my life exposed for examination. They are precious little miracles (some of them are not so little, either!) handed to us as gifts we lose too easily. The journals allowed me to stand back from both dreams and coincidences, to see them from the proper perspective of time.

The eerie sensation of that nameless awe that attended the Rushdie-car experience descended on me again, but it was even heavier than before. I had to break off reading after only a few minutes, so overwhelming was the numinous atmosphere I felt around me. It was a kind of rapture I thoroughly grasped with something other than my rational mind—a dawning awareness or certainty, like something that had always rumbled darkly in some subconscious cavern but had not been consciously recognized until that instant. It was one of those "Ah-ha!" moments, when the self-evidence of a great truth suddenly stands before us revealed in all its potent significance.

Eventually recovering myself, I returned to the journals and read them through, marveling in the deepest astonishment at page after page of the unaccountable events that were the core experiences of a life I no longer felt to be entirely my own. Finally putting them aside, I felt as though I had just read a new Book of Revelation more personally meaningful than anything previously known. Yet I was aware at the same moment that this heightened recognition of acausal events signified a universal principle and belonged to every human being in the world. The synchronicities that happened to me were like fingerprints: Everybody has them, but each individual possesses a unique set. Anyone who keeps a close record of personal coincidences over time will experience the same revelation I did.

I needed a quiet time alone in which to mentally digest the impact of my self-discovery and to make plausible deductions from it, if I dared. The implications of my journals, written in total ignorance of their real contents, subverted my rational understanding of existence and, more alarming, hinted at a direct hookup with the Great Unknown Mystery itself. Unaccompanied, I fled from the Twin City region of Minnesota, across the country into the Rocky Mountains of Estes Park. Feeling compelled by the vast silences of its summits, I spent days climbing above the early October snow line, thinking of nothing but feeling much. Still urged on, I drove for days and nights through the West, seeking more silence, a different kind, in the Nevada desert, under the brightest stars I ever saw. Then I crossed the Pacific to Japan, where I joined a best friend, with whom I climbed Mount Fuji. There we witnessed the setting sun and rising moon poised in perfect equilibrium on either side of the volcanic apex, reflecting their combined light from its perpetual icecap. Alone again, I entered the sacred spaces of Thailand's temples, which glittered with millions of gold, red, green, and blue mirrored tiles. There were other holy places, mountains, and deserts—a secluded, ancient Hawaiian temple still revered by local people with platters of fruit; the windblown ridge of Arizona's Meteor Crater, more desert silences at California's Joshua Tree National Park. As in the famous poem, I ran from "the Hound of Heaven."

Temporary escape from the responsibility of systemizing my thoughts provided the clarity and tranquillity of mind I'd lacked in the months before. Protected from the outside world by the arctic spell of a northwestern Wisconsin winter, I calmly began to embrace the task of fitting together the pieces of a cosmic puzzle, the final configuration of which, with an awe verging on appre-hension, I already suspected. As I carefully reexamined not only my own journals but the testimony of all those I interviewed and others whose research I read, the synchronicities began to group themselves into several categories of experience. These ultimately broke down and arranged themselves naturally into seventeen classes that appear common to a broad range of general human encounters with the phenomenon. I have created the categories only for purposes of convenient definition and clarification; they are helpful in understanding the meaning of a particular acausal event. Although these categories run the gamut of psychic phenomena, they go beyond into questions of personal identity, vocation, culture, nature, relationships, character development, and spirituality. Later chapters are dedicated to their descriptions and applications in detail, but their brief definition here will help to introduce a subject as complex as it is fascinating.

My classifications of meaningful coincidence are as follows:

1. *Inanimate Objects.* Some things, manufactured or natural, are perceived as being involved in acausal incidents.
2. *Numbers.* The combination, repetition, or single appearance of numbers can be seen to figure significantly in life and destiny.
3. *Environmental and Animal Ostenta.* Ostenta is a Latin word derived from the Etruscan term for signs or portents in the natural environment that prefigure coming events. Meteorologic, geologic, and biological events sometimes interact with human affairs in ways beyond their material reality.
4. *Premonition.* Premonition is the accurate recognition of an event before it actually occurs.
5. *Dreams (Precognitive and Shared).* Dreams that are pre-cognitive prefigure events that happen in waking life. Shared dreams are those simultaneously experienced by two or more persons.
6. *Telepathy.* The communication between minds through some means other than sensory perception is called telepathy.
7. *Enigmas.* Enigmas may be broken down into numerous subcategories to describe any synchronous episode beyond present understanding or classification.
8. *Origins.* Meaningful coincidences sometimes open up lost information about and connect to individual human origins.
9. *Parallel Lives.* When two or more persons share inex-plicable but meaningful events or characteristics in common, we say they lead "parallel lives."
10. *Life Imitates Art.* Art is an important connecting agent in itself and sometimes touches all the other categories.
11. *Warnings.* Coincidences that intervene against danger fall in the category of warnings.
12. *Death.* A subcategory of precognition, death is among the most common and important foreseen events that occur in acausal conditions.
13. *Rescue.* Rescue is the timely arrival of acausal events that help avoid danger.

14. *Reincarnation.* Reincarnation is the belief that the soul leaves after the body's biological death to be reborn in another physical form as part of its development.
15. *Guidance.* Some synchronicities act as guidance for personal improvement.
16. *Moira.* A Greek word commonly understood and esteemed during the golden age of classical philosophy more than two thousand years ago, when Athens was the learning center of the civilized world, *moira* signifies the "higher calling" available to every man and woman, their real life's work, not necessarily (nor usually) the job they perform in order to earn a living wage.
17. *Transformational Experiences.* The category of transformational experiences encompasses life-changing coincidences and/or personal links with a spiritual dimension.

The chief utility of these inclusive categories is to group a particular meaningful coincidence with its own kind. From this common base, we have several reference points from which we may begin making conclusions. Unlocking the symbolic codes of synchronicities is important, because they are, in effect, highly personal messages we all receive for our own good. Their intense individuation—their very nature as personalized phenomena—make such incidents best interpreted by the person who experiences them. A do-it-yourself process for decoding synchronicity is spelled out in chapter 9. Their meaning is not always readily apparent, and if one does not take steps to preserve the message, it may quickly fade like invisible ink. Without the interpretive method presented in these pages, the overall effect of a series of coincidences in one's life might be lost, their purport vanishing with them. Moreover, classification, by its very multiplicity, tends to lend credence to the synchronicity phenomenon. As Jung himself believed, "The numinosity of a series of chance happenings grows in proportion to the number of its terms" (Jung, p. 33).

Those who shared their acausal experiences with me were not always interested in determining the core meanings or origins of unaccountable events. Many people felt these were too mysterious to grasp. While these individuals accepted synchronicity as miraculous, they were mostly content to value it as a form of guidance. A common assessment of the phenomenon was, "Whenever a meaningful coincidence happens to me, I feel I am doing the right thing, or, in an opposite situation, I am being warned, and that's all I need to know." But when offered new techniques for the interpretation of their encounters, these same people wanted to learn how these techniques could be used.

Means to interpret synchronous events have not been seriously proposed for the last 1,600 years. Before then, the adepts of various mystery religions revered them as messages from the gods and were supposed to possess the expertise necessary for decoding them. But, being sworn to secrecy under pain of death, these diviners were allowed to share their knowledge with fellow initiates only. The ancient mysteries were teachings about the relationship between man and creation, principles considered too esoteric and sacred for public consumption, and imparted to students in a series of revealing initiations. When these cults were outlawed and aggressively suppressed by successive Christian emperors, their secrets vanished with them.

The *Disciplina Etrusca* perhaps violated the standard proscription against going public with esoteric information. This book was an encyclopedia of divination compiled by the Etruscans, pre-Roman inhabitants of west-central Italy, who were intensely interested in synchronous phenomena. Like most of the literature of the ancient world, the *Disciplina Etrusca* was lost with the fall of classical civilization. Even a volume written about Etruscan religion by the erudite Emperor Claudius failed to survive. A few fragments of mutilated works by other Roman writers were preserved, and from these, historians have been able to piece together something of the original. Along with their magnificent cities of splendid temples, frescoed mausoleums, and superb bronzework, the Etruscans developed systems for the close examination of nature in which they detected omens pertinent to the destiny of mankind. Certain details in a flight of birds, a flash of lightning, or an earthquake presaged the shape of things to come in a language of symbols meaningful to human beings.

Far from having been the ludicrous superstition of a backward race, the *Disciplina Etrusca* represented the spiritual epitome of an unquestionably great people. Their other achievements in art, architecture, astronomy, seamanship, irrigation, and city planning are as admired today by scholars as they were by the Romans, who eventually conquered and absorbed their civilization. The few details of sixth-century B.C. divination that survived the demise of the classical world suggest that the Etruscan adepts regarded meaningful coincidence as the active principle of their interpretations. Chapter 10 of *Synchronicity & You* returns to the ancient origins of humankind's attempts at understanding the significant intervention of acausal events. The Etruscans are mentioned here only because they, with one exception (also cited in chapter 10), seem to have solved the mystery of synchronicity more successfully than virtually all the philosophers and psychologists who have grappled with it since Schopenhauer and Jung.

The ancient Etruscans appear to have concluded, after literally generations of documented observation, that the physical universe and everything in it, inanimate and organic, from the smallest detail to the largest objects and clusters of objects, are all interconnected by an unseen organizing power that establishes and enforces certain general laws. They traced this organizing power using simple examples, such as the individual leaf with its purposeful design replicated thousands of times on the branches of a tree, itself a complexly designed natural phenomenon intimately related to the forest of other trees in which it stands, and no less closely tied in with the nutritious earth below and the life-giving rains from above. Nor is this the end of a closed cycle, because the tree produces fruit eaten by animals, some of which are human, whose lives are sustained by the fruit and whose own droppings renurture the soil, while carrying seeds of the tree to take root and prosper elsewhere, thereby perpetuating and expanding the pattern. The metaphor may be infinitely extended and broadened to include the entire universe: the sun that gives life to the tree, the gases from which the sun coalesced, the origin of these gases from an earlier star, and so forth, *ad infinitum*, beyond human ken. An interrelationship and interdependence of details is inextricably bound up with every step of the analogy.

The Etruscans believed that the organizing power of the universe was invisible and unknowable. But they also inferred from its observable effect on all things that it unified matter in an infinity of purposes that accumulated into a single, overriding purpose—namely, to go on reaching ever higher levels of refined organization, not in a linear progression but through recurring cycles, building greater strength with the completion of each revolution. For the Etruscan adepts, an unseen (although visible in its effects) parallel sphere of existence underlay and interpenetrated the material universe. It not only organized all natural phenomena but was intimately involved with thought and destiny, as proved by episodes of meaningful coincidence, in both human and nonhuman affairs. Accordingly, the Etruscans made a science of observing the interrelated nuances of nature and human behavior. Paying attention to such synchronous phenomena and consciously relating them to their lives helped their vibrant society to prosper for nearly five hundred years.

Materialist admirers of the pre-Roman civilizers otherwise dismiss the *Disciplina Etrusca* as so much superstitious rubbish. Responding to modern criticism of the ancient world's *magnum opus* on spiritual matters would deflect from the more immediate intent of our discussion. But as a point of appropriate synchronicity, it is intriguing to know that the Etruscans commonly used a sheep's liver or a bronze pallet configured like one for divination purposes, because they believed this organ most resembled the shape of the universe. By the late 1990s, astrophysicists compiling a virtual avalanche of new data from the Hubble space telescope and related Earth-orbiting sources compared the deduced shape of the universe to a sheep's liver. Coincidence? Yes, but a meaningful one, and that is what synchronicity is all about. Or perhaps the Etruscans knew more about the universe than we imagine they did.

While not allowing our discussion of synchronicity to become mired with digressions into philosophy and history, it is nevertheless vital to at least appreciate what happened to this lifeline between the individual human soul and the world soul and why it continues to be largely neglected today. Meaningful coincidence appears to have been the kernel of all the higher spiritual disciplines practiced in the ancient world, when its numerous manifestations were regarded as various kinds of omens.

Nor was its primal importance grasped only in the West. Mesoamerican religion recognized synchronous events connecting humankind to the natural world, as epitomized in the Mayas' highly sophisticated understanding and social application of astronomical cycles. The Maya legacy was passed down to subsequent pre-Columbian peoples, such as the Aztecs. From its towering position atop a huge, white pyramid at the splendid city of Tenochtitlán, the Aztec's enormous Calendar Stone loomed. Its name is a modern misnomer. The twelve-foot-tall, twenty-four-ton stone disk was actually a sculpted, brightly painted almanac, the artistic rendering on a colossal scale of an astral computer known to ancient Americans as the Vessel of Time. Its dominant position at the Aztecs' capital was meant to synchronize their lives, individually and as a society, with the cycles of life punctuated by extraordinary events analogous to meaningful coincidences.

In July 1543, this monumental work of art, science, and spirituality was pried from its base under the orders of Spanish friars who condemned it as "Satan's platter." They sent it careening across the grand staircase of Tenochtitlán's pyramid to crash facedown in the street. The same benighted spirit of destruction had begun its work a thousand years earlier with the demonization of pagan Europe. The triumph of a Dark Age mentality in the fifth century straitjacketed Western thought by instituting a clear, irrevocable distinction between matter and spirit. God and humans, heaven and earth, body and soul were rigidly defined by a duality of mutually exclusive opposites, a duality preached as dogma that dominated European thinking from that time to the present.

As the twig is bent, so grows the tree, and even philosophy and science were stunted by this simplistic world view. René Descartes split nature into two hostile camps of mind and matter, while Sir Isaac Newton carried Cartesian dualism to its logical extreme by reducing the entire universe to a soulless machine. European religion, philosophy, and science insisted that humans were something apart from nature, an attitude resulting in environmental havoc that continues to subvert the ecological basis of life on earth. When the first modern Europeans came to America and beheld its astounding natural panorama, they were primarily excited by the apparently limitless wealth that was theirs for the taking. In their dehumanized view of the world, the forests, prairies, and Native Americans were indifferently swept aside in the name of profit, because the newcomers had been indoctrinated for centuries with the belief that the Earth was an inanimate object to be exploited wherever possible. In Wisconsin alone, by the turn of the twentieth century, nearly all of the state's pine forests were reduced to timber, leaving behind a ravaged landscape. One awful consequence of this exploitation was the Dust Bowl catastrophe of the 1930s.

Although vastly outnumbered by majority opinion, dissenting voices against Europe's intellectual medievalism began to make themselves heard as early as the seventeenth century with Leibnitz. Since his time, the decline of an all-pervasive religious dogma has been accompanied by developments in atomic physics, which reveal the serious limitations and incompleteness of the Newtonian model of the universe. With growing understanding of the space-time continuum, physicists observed the interchange of matter and energy at the levels of atomic particles. Incredibly, even the physicist himself interacts on an energy level with his own exper-iment. No less decisively, Jung, the pioneering psychologist, demonstrated humankind's subconscious kinship with all living and inanimate matter. Likewise, Joseph Campbell, the mythologist, showed that this kinship has been recognized and venerated by human beings everywhere from deeply prehistoric times, surviving into the present mostly in Asian belief systems. These ideas were forcefully and poetically stated in Campbell's famous series of published research, *The Masks of God*.

Today, science is on the side of synchronicity as a unifying phenomenon, and you will no longer be burned at the stake for stating publicly that meaningful coincidences are your personal con-nection with the World Soul. You may lose your job for volunteering such an opinion, and other people might avoid being seen in your presence. But you will at least be free to pursue the mystery and meaning of the significant coincidences that guide and form your life, synchronicities no one may appreciate better than yourself. The following chapters will help you to gain that appreci-ation.

chapter 2

Signs of the Times in Objects and Numbers

I feel yet cannot understand it. I cannot grasp it, but can't forget it either. And if I think I've completely gotten hold of it, I am unable to measure it! So how can I possess something that seems immeasurable? It fits no rule, and yet it is flawless.

—Hans Sachs in Act II, Scene 3,
The Mastersingers of Nuremberg, by Richard Wagner

Moments of synchronicity are often so fleeting and elusive they are difficult for us to grasp. We experience their dramatic sense of connection but do not always understand them. Meaningful coincidence is not one single thing. There are many different types of synchronicity. My research has suggested certain fundamental categories into which all synchronous events fall. These categories should be understood as useful parameters for identifying the specific kind of synchronous event under investigation. Once an acausal episode has been classified and the nature of its type understood, the next step, decoding it, may be taken. Nor are such categories strictly compartmentalized, one category clearly defined from another. The boundaries separating them are indefinite. Elements from one group may spill over and merge with others, blurring any sharply focused distinctions. Indeed, all the classifications presented here are consociated members of the same synchronicity family. It may help to realize that they are but variations on a common theme.

Synchronicity & You is a manual for practical definitions and applied use. Its various categories are informally organized into groupings of similar kinds of experience. Throughout, my intent has been to simplify and clarify a complex phenomenon, to remove it from the scientific and philosophical jargon that has prevented personally meaningful coincidences from being appreciated by general readers. The following classifications will provide us with a clear overview of synchronicity in many of its varied aspects. We will learn how synchronous events influence individual human affairs in ways deemed almost magical. More important, we should find a categorical niche for our own meaningful coincidence and, at the same time, a starting point for unraveling its significance.

Inanimate Objects

John Miller has been a record collector since his early youth; his vinyl, CD, and tape library is enormous, and it keeps growing. For him, life without his private preserve of music and spoken-word recordings would not be worth living. But one piece of music had long eluded him. It was the sound track to a CBS television-series broadcast during the early 1960s narrated by actor Robert Ryan. Entitled *World War One*, it was a collection of old film footage organized into a seven-part documentary. But it was the haunting, evocative music composed for the program by Morton Gould that lingered in the memory of the record collector.

Despite years of inquiry, Miller had not been able to find a copy of the sound track. As far as he was able to determine, no commercial recording of it had ever been issued. A full quarter of a century after the series had been aired and virtually forgotten, a business trip took him to Lansing, Illinois. Finding himself with an hour to spare before his appointment, he absentmindedly cruised the few bins of circulating records at the local public library. As he did so, an eerie certainty came over him of a kind he had never felt before. "I am going to find the sound track to *World War One*," he thought to himself, but he almost immediately reacted against his nonsensical intuition. Such a record did not even exist. Not one minute later, he found a copy of the original musical sound track. He was thunderstruck by the experience. All the years between then and his adolescence, when he had seen the program and enjoyed its music, seemed magically bridged in that wonderful moment. He remembered his feeling of sure anticipation moments before his find but could not understand how he had known what would happen.

Not long after his discovery, he was at a special sale in a downtown Chicago record store where literally tens of thousands of records were stacked in unmarked crates. Everything was on sale in a catch-as-catch-can discount after inventory. Looking over the vast chaos of records, Miller shuddered with the same kind of certainty he had experienced in Lansing. "I'm going to find a rare recording of John Barrymore I don't even know exists," he thought to himself. This time, he did not resist the feeling but chose to randomly rummage through a colossal stack of records. After going through fewer than a dozen, he found *John Barrymore on the Radio*, an album that featured material never released before or since.

Miller has no control over his precognitive sensations. He cannot will them into action and deliberately go hunting for rare records. Instead, the feeling comes to him of its own accord. All he does is cooperate with it by opening himself to its guidance and following where it prompts him. The kind of synchronicity he experiences connects him with inanimate objects—in his case, recordings. While the irregular repetitiveness of his experience may not be all that common, many people recall duplicating similar acausal finds of their own at least once in their lives, in a magical discovery of some special object of desire.

Parapsychologist Alan Vaughn, while a college student struggling to earn his tuition at a part-time job at the Akron Public

Library, very much wanted to possess the nine Beethoven symphonies then newly released in a deluxe set of records featuring the renowned Arturo Toscanini with the NBC Orchestra. The set was far beyond his own financial means at the time, but he obtained the album for a friend who placed an order through the library. When it arrived, Vaughn was amazed to see that two sets had been sent accidentally, although there was a bill for only one. The other was a gift of providence to the poor college student who loved music (p.75).

Vaughn also reported the story of a woman who wanted to obtain a special arrangement of Antonín Dvořák's *Humoresque* for her elderly father at Christmastime. The version he most enjoyed was for violin and piano, but a clerk at the local record store informed her that no recordings of the piece performed by these two instruments were currently available, all such renditions having long before gone out of print. A few weeks before Christmas, the same clerk was surprised to receive a recorded copy of *Humoresque* for violin and piano—surprised because the store had not placed an order for a recording everyone believed was out of print. Moreover, in an unheard-of mix-up, it bore a label different from that of the company that had unaccountably sent it. In view of these extraordinary events, the store presented the record free of charge to the woman, whose father received a perfect, logically impossible, Christmas gift (Vaughn, p. 73).

Here, in fact, is a key to understanding at least part of the mechanism involved in psychic location: The person must be deeply, even passionately, devoted to the item. It is absolutely of no consequence that the interested—perhaps even obsessed—person is almost entirely ignorant of its existence or even many of its particulars. Often, the less one consciously knows about the object, the better the chances of coming into contact with it, because the subconscious is less distracted by the half-truths of the rational mind. All that matters is that the person be intensely interested in the inanimate object. It is this high level of emotional involvement that activates synchronicity. The record collector built up a tremendous degree of interest over his quarter-of-a-century longing for the sound track of *World War One*. He was also a longtime admirer of John Barrymore. These recordings were deeply meaningful to him and added immeasurably to the quality of his life. But only recordings of this highest personal significance came to him through synchronicity. The acausal principle never brought him to works he cared about less, no matter how valuable or desirable they were.

Another incident serves to demonstrate that such connections occur with simple objects. For no apparent reason, a middle-aged man began recalling his early university days with fondness, when he had moved away from the home of his parents for the first time and lived alone in the rented room of a distant boarding house. For the first time in more than thirty years, he remembered with affection a simple oil lamp made of stained glass that used to stand on his desk. An inexpensive item he purchased at a local department store, it nevertheless helped to create a charming atmosphere in his otherwise bare, small room. It contributed, marginally if indelibly, to happy memories of his youth. When he left school, the lamp was mislaid and not seen again. In the decades of life that followed, it was forgotten, but, without obvious cause, the memory of it began to resurface with his bout of nostalgia.

Shopping around for an identical replacement, he found none and was informed that small lamps of the kind he'd once possessed had not been manufactured for a very long time. In fact, they were now so rare that some people were paying ten and even twenty times their original cost when they found such lamps. He assumed he would never see the likes of his desk lamp again. But one day he was visiting a friend's home when he noticed to his astonishment that the very object of his fond memory was sitting before him on a table. It was identical to the little stained-glass oil lamp he had not seen in over thirty years. Noticing the man's interest, his friend presented it to him as a gift.

In this example of synchronicity, desire was the mechanism connecting man and item. But the inanimate object was more than a material thing. On a conscious level, it was his link with a happy period of his youth. On a higher, archetypal level, the lamp was a symbol of learning associated with his burgeoning young mind during early years at the university. The term *archetype* was coined by Carl Jung. He defined archetypes as symbols common to all humanity. They are subconscious images rooted in our "collective

unconscious," expressed in art and religion, and loaded with transformational significance. From ancient times, lamps have signified
the search for wisdom and truth, dispelling the darkness of
ignorance with enlightenment. Thus understood in its archetypal
context, finding the lamp through synchronicity meant that the man
was bringing an old light to bear on his past when, as a young
student, he was pursuing his education.

Appropriately enough, the lamp is a traditional symbol of
intelligence or enlightenment. Interestingly, it also appears among
the tarot deck, a set of divination cards, as the Hermit. The
Hermit's position in the Ninth Enigma depicts him carrying a
lantern partially covered by one of the folds of his cloak, signifying
the concealing darkness of ignorance from which light emerges.
The Hermit represents tradition, study, reserve, patience, and
profound work leading toward enlightenment. Recall that the man
seeking the stained-glass lamp associated it with a period of happy
solitude in the school boarding house. All these archetypes,
universal human images connecting our collective unconscious
with some Super Consciousness, were at work in the synchronicity
that brought the man and his lamp together. And they suggest that
its reappearance in his middle-aged life meant something more
than satisfying nostalgic longing for a lost youth. The lamp that
signified an earlier period of education was remanifesting itself
much later as an indication that the time had come again for the
man to seek enlightenment—that true education does not end with
one's school days but must go on in the greater university of the
world, regardless of one's age. Had he been preached at with such
an obvious truth, he might have dismissed it as unsolicited advice.
But the powerful personal symbolism of the rediscovered lamp,
entering his life when it did, affected him more deeply than
anything his closest friends could have told him.

In a case of synchronicity upon synchronicity, I was one day
thinking absentmindedly about a European surplus army moun-
taineer's cap I'd bought at a fair several years before and liked to
wear often. A few minutes later, I began reading the latest issue of
a magazine that carried a report about Roger Nussbaumer, who
ordered an Alpine cap through a mail-order military supply house.
He had some weeks before browsed through its catalog, where he

found a photograph of the same kind of headgear he once wore as a young recruit in the Third Company, First Troop of the Swiss army. More out of nostalgia than necessity, he ordered one of the caps. The army surplus supply house had three thousand such hats for sale. Yet, the used cap Mr. Nussbaumer received still had a label inside reading, "R. Nussbaumer, Co. 3, Troop 1," in his own hand-writing; it was the very cap he'd worn in the service (O'Neill, p. 5).

The meaningful coincidences cited in this section demonstrate that such events do not have to be hugely life-changing or over-whelmingly transformational to qualify as genuine instances of synchronicity. In fact, the vast majority of acausal incidents are rela-tively low-key. That is why people overlook them so easily and fail to appreciate their significance.

Numbers

Numbers often serve as vehicles for meaningful coincidence. To paraphrase Jung, numbers are archetypes of order that have become conscious. Critics may object that numbers are entirely the abstract product of the human mind, nothing more than quantifying concepts that did not exist before being invented. But Jung and others, going back to the Pythagoreans of early classical Greece, believed numbers were as much found as invented. They represent the form and rhythm of the universal order interpenetrating and organizing matter.

A common numerical synchronicity involves digits that repeat themselves with a significance more often felt than understood. A case in point occurred during a lecture I gave some years ago at a local meeting of the Society for the Advancement of Research and Enlightenment, also known as the Edgar Cayce organization. During the course of my presentation, I discussed the esoteric meaning of the number six, as it was used by Plato in his dialogue the *Kritias*. In Plato's symbolic progression of numbers, one repre-sented the primal cause of creation; two, its division into the sacred duality structuring the universe (light/dark, hot/cold, hard/soft, and so on); three, the unity of the primal cause with the sacred duality resulting in God/Goddess, the Creator/Creatoress; four, the balance

He/She achieves through the harmonization of opposites manifested in the sacred androgyne (Eros, the Christ child, and so on); and five, the masculine principle of dynamic action. Six, according to Plato, stood for the eternal feminine, the nurturing principle of receptivity. To the Pythagoreans who preceded him and the Cabalists who came after, six was sacred to the goddess of love, Venus, "and thus it is regarded as an ideal love number" (Kozminsky, p. 19). It was associated with feminine abundance.

After the talk, I was approached by a woman from the audience in a condition of obvious excitement. She had come to my lecture about the legend of Atlantis, not expecting to learn anything about numerical symbolism, but she said I had unwittingly provided her with a transformational experience in describing the ancients' esoteric view of the number six. For the past several years, she explained, her attention had been constantly called to this number. It seemed to appear everywhere, all the time, as though insisting she take notice of it: six letters would arrive on the sixth day of the sixth month; she once discovered six pennies at 6:00 P.M. just as the six o'clock news came on Channel 6. She usually found herself sixth in line at the supermarket, and her bills often involved divisions of six. She once saw six birds sitting together on a tree branch outside her window. If she noticed children playing outside, there were usually six of them together. Whenever she happened to glance at her watch, it was six minutes before or after the hour. She would turn on the radio and the first spoken word was often "six." Books always seemed to open to a sixth chapter or a sixth page. In otherwise normal conversations, she was often asked questions or told things involving the number six by people who knew nothing of the number's recurrence in her life: Was it the sixth inning of a baseball game? My daughter just finished sixth grade. Please make six copies of this report. The number was proclaiming itself everywhere, from license plates and marquees to boxes of laundry detergent and television commercials. Everyday examples were commonplace events. But it was their incessant occurrence that she could not fail to notice.

While at first she was amused by the phenomenon, the perplexity of it made her feel that, in her own words, "Somebody was trying to tell me something. What it was, I could not figure out. I began asking friends what they thought was happening to me. Most were as mystified as myself. Some told me I should be careful; that something might be threatening me. One person said that Satan was after me, because the Devil's number is supposed to be 666."

But she did not feel that there was anything ominous about her "numerical run-ins," and she utterly rejected the notion of receiving overtures from Beelzebub. There was, nevertheless, a quality or nuance of urgency about the persistence of the number. She noticed that it began to call her attention, sporadically at first, although with growing frequency over time, at a juncture in her life when she was unable to decide between marriage and a career. In her case, the two were not compatible. After she heard my lecture, the increasing repetition of the number six struck her with the full force of its meaning. She believed it was telling her to reemphasize her femininity, to choose a husband over an employer.

Even the fact that she attended the lecture was synchronous, because she intuitively felt before arriving at the meeting hall that she would learn something vitally important, although she had no idea at the time what it might be. The rest of my presentation had been totally subordinated in her estimation to Plato's associations with the number six, which explained why this number had been pestering her at this particular period in her life. With this revelation, the woman confessed to a wonderful, soulful feeling of release and recognition mixed with the sensation of Otherworldly guidance. Interestingly, while she thereafter continued to regard it with special favor, she no longer met with the number in the same kind of significant patterns that seemed to demand notice before her decision to marry.

This example of number synchronicity is typical of such experiences, in that anyone thus confronted by the repetition of a number invariably feels that something important, perhaps even divine, is trying to communicate through the numerical symbol. As one of the greatest mathematicians of all time, the eighteenth-century German genius Karl Friedrich Gauss, proclaimed, "God arithmetizes!" By this he meant that numbers were not man-made conventions to measure the immeasurable universe, but were implicit in the organizing principle found throughout creation.

The woman's meaningful coincidence likewise demonstrates that the individual best qualified to decode its symbolism is the person to whom it is given. Just as we would rather not have someone else read for us the letters we receive from loved ones, so we are quite capable of reading the communiqués of meaningful coincidence without outside assistance. *Synchronicity & You* provides helpful guidelines and useful categories to bring the phenomenon into focus, but it cannot and should not presume to interpret acausal events for anyone. The final word of interpretation rests with the person to whom the synchronicity has been given.

Perhaps more than any other numeral, six is involved in meaningful coincidences that reflect its symbolism. Another similar example took place on Halloween, 1996. At that time, 436 persons chose the numbers 666 in the Wisconsin Daily Pick 3 lottery. They deliberately selected this set as an appropriate amusement, recalling that it is popularly associated with Satan. The 436 Wisconsinites who played 666 that special night won an unprecedented $178,000. According to lottery officials, that amount was an unheard-of 4.5 times the average payout.

But these numerical encounters were not unique. The life of Pope Pius X (1835–1914), for example, was divided into time periods of nine. He was a curate for nine years and spent nine years as a parish priest, nine years as a bishop, nine years as an archbishop, and nine years as the patriarch of Venice. His feast day was in September, the ninth month and the month in which he made his most important decisions, such as the 1910 edict commanding that all teachers in seminaries and clerics before ordination take an oath denouncing "modernism"—an act that shook the Roman Catholic Church to its ecumenical foundations. Officers in the Church were aware of the strange ninefold symbolism surrounding Pius X. While he was secluded with a serious illness in 1912, rumors of his death began to circulate. But Australia's Monsignor Phelan assured readers of the *Melbourne Herald* that His Holiness would surely survive, because "on August 1st he will have completed his ninth year as Pope." Pius X lived another two years, dying in the ninth year of his seventh decade.

But the number nine also demonstrates the degree to which such symbolism is subjective and how susceptible it is to different, personal interpretations. Among some musicians it is regarded as death's own number. This negative association began with Beethoven, who died after completing his ninth symphony. Following the lethal pattern he apparently set, many of the world's leading composers expired after composing their own ninth symphonic works. Anton Bruckner, Antonín Dvořák, Ralph Vaughan Williams, and Alexander Galzunov are the best-known examples. Long oppressed by what he felt was the heavy hand of inevitable fate and keenly aware of the lethal numerical symbolism facing him, Gustav Mahler raced to complete a tenth symphony and thereby break the ominous pattern. But he failed. At fifty years of age, he died, and his Ninth Symphony remains his final completed work.

Jean Sibelius, having written the final note to his Eighth Symphony, did not ignore the traditionally dark numerical symbol associated with a ninth symphony. When the publisher who contracted with him for the work arrived at his home to collect the score, he was shown to a veranda facing the backyard. Sibelius was busily engaged at an outdoor stove, where he had just burned each page of his latest work into a pile of ashes. The Finnish maestro's Eighth Symphony was never heard. He admitted that feelings of foreboding made him uneasy whenever he contemplated ideas for the following symphony, a ninth. Sibelius wanted to put a feeling of "distance" between himself and that traditionally fatal work. He lived long past his ninety-first birthday.

The London musicologist Piers Burton-Page wrote in his program notes for Britain's late-twentieth-century composer Malcolm Arnold, "There has come to be something fatalistic about the very idea of a ninth symphony." He mentions that Soviet composer Dimitri Shostakovich was "over-awed by the burden of this musical tradition." Sir Malcom, too, became part of the fatalistic tradition when he completed his Symphony Number Nine, his last.

In esoteric symbolism, the number nine does exemplify art through the nine muses.

Otto von Bismarck, Germany's "Iron Chancellor," acknowledged that he had inherited the number three as the lucky talisman of his life from his ancestors. His family coat of arms was the trefoil with three oak leaves (themselves symbols of victory).

Bismarck served three emperors, fought and won three wars, signed three victorious peace treaties, formed the Triple Alliance that ensured the Reich's dominant position in Europe, controlled three political parties, and engineered modern Europe's first high-level summit of three emperors to create a lasting peace. He also sired three children and owned three estates.

Perhaps because of its venerable associations with godhood (from Neptune's trident to the Christian Trinity), the number three has generally been considered lucky, although only individuals with the willpower of Bismarck seem able to take full advantage of its fortunate aspects. But add three to ten, and the result becomes three's symbolic antithesis. The reasons for this are older and more complex than those assigned to Judas, the thirteenth dinner guest at the Last Supper. Thirteen's unfortunate connotations go back to Norse, Roman, Hindu, and even Mesoamerican myth. As Kozminsky wrote, "This superstition seems to be very universal and is of very ancient origin" (pp. 35, 36).

The number thirteen also plays a part in synchronicity. According to his autobiography, John Millais, the great Pre-Raphaelite painter, threw a dinner party in August 1885 for his equally renowned friend, the poet Matthew Arnold. One of the guests, noticing that there were thirteen persons assembled at the table, expressed some misgivings that, according to tradition, the first to absent themselves from the gathering would be dead within a year. The robust Arnold, declaring his intention of personally debunking this superstition, deliberately walked out together with two companions as the first to leave. Half a year later, Arnold died of a surprise heart attack. One of his defiant friends committed suicide within the same week, while the other companion drowned at sea the following February (Kozminsky, p. 37).

Interpreters of these synchronous deaths might point out that there was nothing supernatural about the number thirteen. Instead, it was an archetypal symbol for the unseen spiritual dimension underlying and organizing the entire material universe. In other words, invisible power is to the physical world what our thoughts are to our bodies. When Arnold and his fellow dinner guests delib-erately denied the reality of the world's spiritual power, it affirmed its own existence by taking theirs.

The case of Wolfgang Pauli demonstrates that fatality is not confined to thirteen and yet shows how numbers do figure into the synchronicity of death. Like Jung, Pauli was an early investigator of meaningful coincidence, and he won the Nobel Prize for Physics in 1945 for his discovery of the Pauli Exclusion Principle, which states that no two electrons in an atom can exist at the same time in the same state or configuration, thereby accounting for the observable patterns of light that atoms emit. This was important because it made clear the reason for the structure of the periodic table of elements. For much of his career, Pauli was perplexed by a complex problem in modern physics (the fine structure constant) that involves the number 137. Despite his best efforts, a solution continued to elude him, as it still does modern scientists. On being admitted to a Zurich hospital for an apparently non-life-threatening ailment in his fifty-eighth year, he was shocked to see the room into which he was being moved. He confided to visitors, "I will never get out of here." He was right. Pauli died in Room 137 (Peat, p. 22). Pauli's case, like many others, reveals that the recipient of synchronicity is its best interpreter. To anyone else, the number 137 would have meant nothing.

People have associated death with certain numbers or their arrangement since ancient times. This association continues to be popularly expressed when people speak of someone who died because "their number was up."

The foregoing personal cases illustrate certain human responses to particular numbers and their inherent symbolism as links to synchronicity. In their progression from one through nine, numbers esoterically tell the story of the spiritual development of the World Soul from beginning to ultimate manifestation. At the beginning of this section I explained what the numbers one through six represent. Seven signifies the completion of cycles, as found in the seven colors of the rainbow, the seven major chakras, the seven days of the week, worldwide tales of the seventh son of a seventh son, and more. Eight is associated with sacrifice and the dissolution of physical forms in life's fundamental process to renew itself. It is symbolized by the eight-legged spider, which, in its ceaseless alternation of web-weaving and killing, continuously oscillates between life and death. Nine, because it is the triple synthesis of three—the

God number—stands for immortality, the ultimate conquest of death, and the culmination of the eight previous numerical symbols, which is the attainment of divinity. All subsequent numbers are variants and elaborations based on one through nine. Ten, for example, is twice five—representing the male principle—and therefore represents kingship or domination in the material world.

In addition to the cases described above, individuals in my survey group told of their synchronistic encounters with certain numbers that connected with significant moments in their lives. Father Robert Handrick, a Catholic priest and scholar of Christian mysticism, recounted how he was confronted at virtually every turn with the number four over the course of several months following Christmas of 1958. Friends were constantly bringing up the number in conversation; he kept noticing its appearance on billboards and license plates; it seemed that every time he turned on the radio he heard only quartets; he was always fourth in line at the super-market; and so forth. The number was relentless in its attempt to capture his attention.

Some library research revealed that the esoteric significance of four lay in the identity of the Sacred Child, so Father Handrick meditated on the image of the Baby Jesus. The previous year had not been an entirely happy one for the priest, mostly because he felt personally uncomfortable in the parish to which he had been assigned and a transfer to a more congenial place seemed out of the question. So, he put on a brave front, cheerfully performed his duties, and never so much as mentioned his true feelings to anyone. Only his meditation on the Christ Child, not surprisingly, brought him a welcome measure of spiritual comfort.

But in mid-March he was astonished to receive a letter from his bishop ordering him to relocate to a parish in the south Chicago suburb of Flossmoor. It was called Infant Jesus of Prague. No less incredibly, the letter specified that Father Handrick's tenure was to begin on April 4—the fourth day of the fourth month. The effect of this multiple synchronicity was profound. Never before had he felt so close to God. His sense of inspirational direction, which he imparted to thousands of parishioners throughout the following decades, never left him. Father Handrick's years at Infant Jesus of Prague were the happiest and most fulfilling of his life, ending in retirement only after he served a lengthy, highly respected term as the head of the congregation.

A less happy but equally cogent numerical synchronicity occurred to the famous Viennese musicologist of the late nineteenth century, Isodore Ochsenschwanz. He was also a noted student of the cabala, the occult Hebrew interpretation of the Old Testament. Combining the two fields of study, Ochsenschwanz was in the process of writing an article about the apparently fatal influence of ninth symphonies on their composers. The elderly scholar was perched high on a rolling ladder among his lofty library shelves when he reached for volume eight in a prodigious set of cabalistic encyclopedias. (While nine seems to be a numeral associated with the terminal works of great symphonic composers, eight is more generally significant of death, as noted earlier, although its real, symbolic implications are not quite so narrow. Coming after seven, the completion of cycles, eight stands for the traditional closing of one door and opening of another. It means *termination*, not *annihilation*; the end of a particular phase, not all phases.) Appropriately, the volume that Ochsenschwanz sought described the lethal significance traditionally associated with this number. As he dislodged the oversized tome, it fell from its shelf, striking Ochsenschwanz and hurling him from the ladder to his death.

Meaningful coincidences involving the number seven are by far the most common in numerical synchronicity, and individuals in our study group reported relatively frequent links between this number and significant events. Audrey Fisher told the story of vacationing with her husband, Barney, at a Las Vegas casino for the first time. After she lost heavily at the slot machines, he refused to give her any more money. In hopes of finding some spare change, she reached into her purse. But all she could scrounge up was $7. Returning with casino coins, she dumped them into the same one-armed bandit that had earlier swallowed all her cash. She then pulled the handle. The numbers that came up did not include seven, but the spate of rattling coins that spewed from the machine amounted to exactly $77. Happy to have won, at least once, the Fishers went home to Indiana.

Interestingly, Fisher's turn of luck through the number seven— popularly associated with good fortune—likewise signaled the end of the couple's vacation at the casino, the completion of a cycle signified by this number. Of course, every serious gambler is a firm believer in the powers of numerical synchronicity and endeavors to put its laws to work for his or her success.

Environmental Ostenta

Ostenta are signs acting as portents in the natural environment that either comment on present circumstances or foreshadow those to come. For the Etruscans, from whom the term derives, ostenta included interpretation of the direction of the wind at a particular moment, the suggestive appearance of a cloud in conjunction with human activity, and the poignant crash of thunder. Even Plato affirmed that an unseen, universe-organizing, spiritual power made itself known in its observable effects on the world of natural phenomena.

Ostenta cover the entire range of natural phenomena, from meteorologic and geologic occurrences to animal behavior—in fact, phenomena involving every living and nonliving thing in the cosmos. If interpreted properly, these acausal incidents in nature reveal what appear to us, from our narrow perspective, to be future events. For synchronicity implies that our linear concept of time, while useful in day-to-day affairs, is only relative to our earthly existence. The universe runs on a different timetable and breaks through to or interfaces with our little human realm only in instances of meaningful coincidence.

Understanding precisely what the omens mean is never easy; it is as difficult a task now as it was in ancient times. When the Roman emperor Augustus was performing an outdoor religious ceremony, a sudden storm blew up, and lightning struck off the C from the motto on the base of a nearby statue of himself. (The letter C is the roman numeral for 100.) Soon after, he became ill and was convinced that he would be dead in one hundred days. A friend visiting him at his sickbed scolded Augustus for not being an expert in the interpretation of signs and pointed out that the obliterated C might just as well mean he had a hundred weeks or even another hundred months left to live. And if it had signified a hundred seconds or minutes, he should have died by this time. Laughing in agreement, Augustus jumped from his sickbed and got back to running the empire for many more years.

His story is valuable because it shows the implicit danger of an incomplete understanding of synchronicity. While the emperor firmly believed in the validity of ostenta, he was, as his friend told him, unskilled in its interpretation. He consequently developed a psychosomatic illness that might very well have undermined his health and killed him within one hundred days, because he was convinced he was not supposed to live any longer.

Actually, his interpretation of the lightning-struck C was entirely incorrect, because the letter had no numerological significance in this case. Instead, the event signified that Augustus would eventually be deified, an unthinkable precedent at the time, but something that nevertheless came to pass when the people and senate of Rome elevated him to "the Divine Augustus." The removal of the C from his statue (by lightning, of all things, the very signature of heavenly intervention in human affairs), left his title reading "aesar," or "of the gods," which was indeed what he became.

Life-changing interpretations of meteorological phenomena are as mystical today as they were in Caesar's time. Married for nearly two years, Richard and Carole Smolinski were trying to have a baby, but the home pregnancy tests they frequently used always came up negative. One day, seemingly the same as all the others, the test again came up negative, but Richard was strangely possessed with euphoric hope for the future. He was traveling to work in this positive state of mind when a high cloud attracted his attention. It had an almost mesmerizing effect on him, and he observed it steadily for about five minutes. As he watched the perfectly ring-shaped cloud floating alone in a blue sky, he felt there was some incomprehensible aura of joy overhead and that his wife would soon give birth to a healthy child. Later that week, the couple's pregnancy test showed positive by displaying a tiny ring floating like a miniature version of the prophetic cloud (Combs and Holland, p. 152).

Smolinski's synchronous experience was a genuine, common instance of ostenta. The irrational joy he felt moments before seeing the cloud, which he intuitively believed signified the birth of a healthy child, was the connecting factor between the same symbol in the heavens and in the pregnancy test. "As above, so below," runs the old motto. It was important, too, that the previously unsure couple needed some assurance that not even a modern pregnancy test could provide. And, in a theme running through most if not all synchronicities, great love and the deepest personal involvement appeared to conjure the experience.

There are a surprising number of people whose sensitivities appear to be in tune with the heavenly spheres. The following provocative, but not unique, case concerned a courier who was part of my research group. In his own words, "While driving home from St. Paul, on the I-90 expressway, around one o'clock A.M., I glanced up at the night sky. It was exceptionally clear, and, for no particular reason, I remembered a very bright meteor I saw while going to school. I hadn't thought of it much since then, and I wasn't especially interested in meteors. Still, the one I saw more than twenty years ago was a beauty. Alone under the autumn sky, except for some light traffic, I wondered if I would ever see another meteor as bright or brighter.

"Maybe fifteen minutes later, I happened to look off to my right, toward the southern hemisphere. I saw a long, intensely brilliant flame of metallic-blue light trailing blue sparks across the moonless sky. At the meteor's center was a bright, metallic-green fire. I wasn't certain, but I thought I could make out some dark object suggested by the fire at its head. The fall lasted a good three seconds and was so impressive I yelled out loud, and my heart beat faster. It was by far the greatest meteor display I've ever seen. At the time, I felt in my heart that I had been presented with some mysterious gift, like a kind of confirmation that I have friends in high places. The whole thing touched me more deeply than I can say."

While out walking with some friends past sunset, the same courier was telling them about his spectacular observation nineteen months before, and he expressed his desire to see another "really extraordinary fireball again." Perhaps three minutes later, a bright-green meteor fell across the area of the sky they happened to be facing. That night's shooting star was second in magnitude only to the one he saw when driving on I-90. On that same expressway, going in the opposite direction, five months later, he was thinking about human beings' untapped spiritual potential, including psychic sensitivity, when the third most dramatic falling star he'd ever witnessed streaked in a long, luminously white light across the western horizon. "I felt deeply," he said, "that the interruption of my thoughts meant that my subconscious picked up somehow on the incoming meteor, but my conscious mind could not understand the information it was getting. Yet, my conscious mind may have been triggered into thinking about spiritual connections with the cosmos, because the subconscious impulse was itself picking up on the shooting star."

Synchronous connections with geological phenomena, particularly earthquakes, seem related to celestial coincidences and are at least as common. Mr. Russell Hooper, a Native American historian in my group who documented his "seismic resonances," as he described them, said he did not always predict an earthquake but more often was aware when one was taking place in some other part of the world. His "resonances" began in his late forties with one of the strangest acausal episodes in his life. On September 21, 1993, he was searching his encyclopedia for information about the Klamath Indians. There were many listings under Klamath, and he was interested only in the Indians, but he could not tear his eyes away from the paragraph on Klamath Falls, in southern Oregon. He was an Illinois resident at the time. "Even after I moved on to another volume of the encyclopedia," he remembered, "I found myself compelled, almost against my will, to go back and stare at the Klamath Falls entry, which I reread at least a dozen times, for no reason I could imagine. The name kept repeating itself in my head like a broken record. And I could not understand why I seemed fixated on a place I had never even heard of or cared about before."

Listening to the news the next morning, he was stunned to learn that Oregon's most powerful earthquake of the century had just occurred, with its epicenter at Klamath Falls. He calculated that the Klamath Falls earthquake took place six hours after his unaccountable obsession with the encyclopedia the previous night. He had not made a prediction, because he had not understood why the mere mention of Klamath Falls exerted such a hold on him.

He'd experienced no sense of anxiety at the time, yet his fixation on Klamath Falls just six hours before the major earthquake there was certainly prescient. Unfortunately, he was unable to properly interpret the coincidental meaning of the Klamath Falls incident.

That earthquake itself had its own curious synchronicity. The tremor dislodged a single boulder, twelve feet in diameter, from the top of a mountain, down which it hurled through the darkness. Simultaneously, a man was driving his pickup truck on a road skirting the same mountain. Driving from his second-shift job along the route he had always taken at the same hour for the past fifteen years, he was oblivious to the twenty-ton menace gathering momentum from above. In an instance of remarkable timing, his truck reached the precise spot in the road where the boulder fell, at the very moment that it fell there. It struck his vehicle in a direct hit that demolished it and instantly killed the driver. Chances against this collision taking place would seem positively astronomical. But when we look beyond mere statistics, we might say that the driver was killed by the unswerving routine into which he placed his life. Such routines are largely regarded in our society as safe and secure. Perhaps a higher power was trying to persuade us otherwise.

Let's return to Hooper, our seismically resonating historian. His distant experience with Klamath Falls alerted him to certain inner potentials that he did not understand but was willing to acknowledge in a nonjudgmental frame of mind. Rather than force or condemn such potentials whenever they seemed to arise, he was determined to follow wherever they led him. His openness resulted in a remarkable vision he had on the night of January 16, 1994, just before falling asleep. He was not dreaming, nor was he fully awake. Instead, he drifted in that twilight zone between full consciousness and sleep. It was in this relaxed condition that a kind of psychodrama began to play out in the back of his mind. "I was walking with some people," he recalled, "a few of whom were leading horses. We were proceeding along a steep mountain trail when suddenly a violent earthquake struck. As the trail rapidly disintegrated down the mountainside, I ran toward a very small stone cave nearby. I literally jumped into it and grabbed onto a kind of small pillar inside. I held on for dear life, while the earth was horribly shaken. I heard some of the other men scream as they fell down the convulsed mountain. After long moments of seismic activity, the quake stopped, and I saw that the trail, horses, men, and all had vanished. Terrified, I wondered how I would ever get out of the tiny cave. End of vision."

As before, a radio announcement the next morning informed him that a major earthquake had taken place. Again, it was remarkable for its magnitude: It was the most powerful of the century to strike Los Angeles. The historian was still living in Illinois, so his simultaneous psychodrama was separated from the actual event by more than fifteen hundred miles and about six hours—the same time period he'd experienced during the Klamath Falls incident. In both cases, his synchronicity connected only with earthquakes of particularly high magnitudes. Yet, his precognition was so abstract in both incidents that he was totally unable to know when, where, or even if an earthquake would occur.

By now, he acknowledged to himself that there was an extra-rational connection between the earth and some part of his mind or soul. He postulated that this connection was the feeble remnant of an innate ability previously developed to a useful level of awareness by precivilized human beings. Those people, living close to nature and cognizant of every nuance in their environment because they had to be to survive, all possessed this ability, but most people lost it when they felt themselves protected by city living. For some reason he didn't understand, a flicker of that ability survived in him. Perhaps continuing to allow it to reassert itself would strengthen whatever fragment of that once universal power he still possessed.

He had to wait until the following September 26 for another recurrence. In the middle of the day, for no apparent cause, he suddenly felt dizzy; the ground seemed to slant away from his feet and he thought immediately, "Earthquake!" But, as before, he could not tell where or when it was taking place. The following day, he read the newspaper report of an earthquake in southern Illinois, along the ominous New Madrid Fault, that occurred at the same moment of his dizzy spell. This time his feelings did not precede the quake, which was a moderate 3.6 on the Richter scale. This encouraged him, because he assumed his sensitivity was increasing. But he experienced no similar earthquake synchronicities until

1995. So many months had passed since the southern Illinois coincidence, in fact, that he had largely forgotten about his innate tie with Mother Earth when he was awakened on the morning of June 15 with the distinct impression of powerful shock waves rising like unthinkable colossal concentric rings from the bowels of the planet. He was somewhat frightened, more awe-inspired, as he thought to himself, "There's an earthquake going on somewhere!" He was right. At the same moment, on the other side of the world, twenty people died in a series of powerful tremors that struck the southern coast of Greece, severely damaging the town of Ezion.

The Greek disaster brought an abrupt change in his attitude toward geologic synchronicity. He began to hate it. As always, he knew something was happening or going to happen somewhere, but he could do nothing to warn anyone. "What good is such a half-ability, if I can do nothing about it?" he despaired. But his sensitivity, as he felt it must be, seemed to grow the following October 20, when he detected a very minor and rare tremor in Minnesota, a state not usually associated with geologic upheavals of any kind. Incredible as it seemed, a quake had indeed taken place there, the first in more than forty years. To an even greater degree than in his past experiences of this kind, the chances of his knowing about this particular event in terms of mere statistical coincidence are beyond calculation.

His first geopsychological experience of 1997 occurred on January 10, while he was living in Monroe, Louisiana. In the early evening, having just taken a hot bath, he was feeling fully relaxed, when a dizziness began to overcome him and the floor of his bedroom seemed to slant away down into the earth; it was the same sensation he'd felt before. "Earthquake again! But where? Where!" he demanded of the unseen provider of geologic information. Strangely, he was answered. He instinctively pointed toward the southwest and felt certain that the epicenter was far away in that direction. "Not very specific, but better than before," he thought. With that, he collapsed into bed, almost overcome with exhaustion. The next day, he heard a news report on the radio of a major earthquake centered far out at sea off the Pacific coast of Mexico.

Since this most recent of his earthquake-oriented synchronicities, Hooper has decided to ask more precisely *when* and *where* the earthquake will take place, rather than simply sensing an earthquake's occurrence. It never occurred to him before to ask such questions, and he feels sure that more answers will be forthcoming. And with answers, he will gain some measure of control. "I have discussed these things with only two other persons, because I do not want to be branded a lunatic or a fraud. No scientist can examine this phenomenon, because I have no idea when it is going to happen. People would just have to take my word for it, and I know that would be asking too much of them. So, I will go about my internal research in silence, alone, wherever it leads. I know there is a connection between myself and earthquake activity, but until I can prove it somehow, I must keep my peace." Only twice has he experienced the sensation of tremors without having been able to verify that earthquakes indeed took place. Even these two apparent lapses in his sensitivity mean little, because the geologic disturbances he felt may have been too slight for mention in the news media.

Apparently acausal human connections with meteorologic or geologic episodes may provide at least a clue to the basis of synchronous phenomena, in that such events tend to demonstrate a very real cause linking both our subconscious and our conscious mind to sudden surges of nature. The difference between modern humans and the natural world may be much smaller than we've thought; our connection with the natural world may be even more intimate. Our very bodies are composed of zinc, copper, iron, seawater, potassium—elements of the Earth. The electrical impulses of our brain resemble flashes of lightning. Our physical relationship with the planet and the elements is close and deep.

Particularly when we see people who experience synchronous events connected to nature, it seems logical to conclude that our total existence is woven into the very fabric of nature, so much so that we have the capacity to feel its every nuance in the same fundamental manner in which we experience the physical reality of our own bodies. The courier whose thoughts anticipated meteors was subconsciously aware of them before his eyes detected their appearance, because he was inwardly attached to the extraterrestrial objects. The Native American historian who senses geologic upheavals is able to do so because his *subconscious* mind and the Earth's *subterranean* mind stand in the same relation to each other as do his physical body and the natural world. They are so intertwined that earthquakes and his physical unease are one and the same sensation. At the very least, if we accept that there is an organic, profoundly personal link between individual human beings and the natural world far beyond our understanding, we can experience a feeling of awe and wonder for our own eternity and cosmic significance.

Animal Ostenta

An animal ostenta is a sign in the form of the coincidental, timely appearance of a creature that connects us with an event of personal significance. To the human psyche, animals are archetypes, powerful symbols representing our instinctual relationship to the world. Synchronicity involving animals is perhaps the most frequent and ancient of ostenta, including members of virtually every living species on the planet. Chief among them are birds. Although usually considered messengers of ill omen, they are not always so. Jung relates an instance of avian synchronicity typical of its kind.

The wife of one of his patients recounted how birds flocked around the windows of the room in which her mother lay dying. Her grandmother's death was accompanied by the same phenomenon. Years later, a medical specialist sent the woman's husband home with a clean bill of health, but when he came home his wife was horrified to see a flock of birds suddenly descend on their house. Aware that similar appearances had coincided with the deaths of her mother and grandmother, she felt the nearness of some impending tragedy. Shortly thereafter, her husband unexpectedly collapsed with a heart attack in the street and was brought home very close to death (Jung, p. 22).

As early as the first century B.C., the Roman statesman Cicero was lying in bed at his summer home in Capiti, when a flock of birds suddenly gathered at his window. This event was regarded by everyone as an ill omen. As Plutarch, his biographer, wrote, "His servants, seeing this, blamed themselves that they should stay to be spectators of their master's murder." That very day, Cicero was assassinated (Plutarch's Lives, p. 110).

In more recent years, one of the men in my survey was reading Homer's *Iliad*. Deeply engrossed in the epic, he read the passage in which the old warrior Nestor rails against his fellow Greeks for their reluctance to face Hector, Troy's greatest soldier. Hector cites Peleus, their national founding father: "If he could hear about them now all trembling before Hector, how he would lift up his hands to heaven and pray that his soul might leave his body and go down to Hades!" At the moment the man came upon that last word, he was startled by the loud thud of a bird colliding with the window, leaving behind as it flew off a single white feather. The man felt compelled to insert this gift between the pages of the pertinent, poignant section. Like all appreciative beneficiaries of synchronicity, he felt much more than he could express, as though some personal connection with the deep past, the nature of the human soul, and a stark comment on his own fortitude had merged simultaneously in a genuinely mystical event of personal significance. That lone white feather, he believed, was a metaphor for the soul.

Birds signify spiritual transition, of which dying is only one kind. They do seem to imply the soul taking leave of its physical home, especially if a window plays some part in their appearance. According to Cirlot, the window expresses penetration and distance, with terrestrial implications, as well as consciousness (p. 27). Hence, the birds, as living metaphors of the soul's flight toward the spiritual Otherworld, beckon through the window of the mundane world, an aperture in our physical existence through which the soul must leave.

The lone eagle is universally regarded as personifying the heights of mystical attainment. As such, it most notably occurs in the Greco-Egyptian phoenix and the Hindu garuda. The former is a symbol of the soul's death and resurrection, while the latter represents its supreme victory over material existence.

Another bird figure personifying the human soul's transformation through the dissolution of physical forms is the owl. It is largely, although not uniformly, perceived as a creature of ill omen, particularly of death. But even this bird is more spiritual than lethal. The North American Kiowa Indians and the Bantu, Zulu, and Yoruba tribes of Africa believe that, after his death, a shaman becomes an owl (Leach, p.142). Interestingly, this concept goes far back into the prehistory of coastal Peru, where the Nazca, civilizers who predated the Incas by fourteen centuries, etched the ninety-eight-foot-tall image of an owl-headed figure into the side of a desert cliff. With its right hand it points at the sky, while its left hand gestures toward the ground, implying the soul's flight from Earth to heaven.

Birds are most commonly associated with premonitions of death when they appear grouped together. According to Cirlot, flocks imply "the collapse of a force" (p.27). Of course, the Etruscan adepts of ostenta believed that to fully understand the message of any such instance of meaningful coincidence, one had to know what kind of bird was involved. When, for example, the boy Claudius Germanicus happened to catch a little puppy dropped from the talons of a huge black eagle flying overhead, a visiting priest who witnessed the incident declared on the spot that the youngster would someday rule Rome. The priest's interpretation was met with general derision, because the lad appeared to be a stuttering moron. Even so, some forty years later, he became Emperor Claudius.

For the Etruscans and their Roman imitators, the appearance of an eagle always portended something pertaining to royal affairs. A woodpecker observed tapping at a temple foretold of coming wars, but a wren building its nest in any structure meant good luck for the inhabitants. White swans were sacred to Sol, the god of light, so their behavior was used in predicting the weather. It is clear that as soon as these ostenta were divested of their intuitive origins by formalized interpretations, they degenerated into superstition.

Bird symbolism began as, and remains, a variegated human archetype that links us to the Otherworld of synchronous phenomena. For example, Donna Foreman, a tourist from the United States visiting Scotland for the first time, set out on a hike one beautiful day in May from the seacoast town of Oban. She wandered inland after some pleasant hours through a lovely valley near an ancient spot called Dalnaneun, or "Place of the Birds." Why it merited that name, she did not know, because, although there were some birds about, nothing in their numbers or behavior suggested anything extraordinary. A few paces beyond Dalnaneun,

Foreman found herself at the foot of Loch Nell, one of the most enchanting places she visited in her travels around the world. Its crystalline water stretched unbroken by a single ripple into the distance between the mountains, while its calm surface mirrored the cobalt-blue sky above. No wind rustled the scented pines.

The loch possessed an absolute peace. Foreman was alone and stretched out on the shore to immerse herself in the singular milieu of this superbly tranquil site. Its remarkable serenity seemed to penetrate to a still-point deep within, until she felt that her very heartbeats, now slow and regular, were in sync with the vibrations of the natural surroundings. Entering into a sense of profound ease, Foreman thought to herself that the picture into which she had wandered was so absolutely perfect that nothing could improve it. No sooner had this feeling expressed itself in her conscious mind then a large white swan, alone and in absolute silence, appeared in the loch. The immaculate apparition cruised across the waveless water, bisecting it with a faint wake between the reflection of twin mountain peaks.

Her thought had been answered by the very environment with which she felt herself in such deep personal harmony. And it had been a whimsical, loving response: "So, you think this is perfectly beautiful? Now watch this!" The spot's name, Place of the Birds, took on special significance for Foreman, who said of her experience, "If I have time to reflect on my life while near death, I will think back to that more-than-perfect moment at the shore of Loch Nell. Its memory will joyfully carry me over from this world to the next, whatever that may be."

Foreman's experience and reaction to it correspond wonderfully with standard interpretations of swan symbolism, which, according to Cirlot, "always points to the complete satisfaction of a desire" (pp.306, 307). He mentions, too, that the swan has been associated with "the mystic Centre," the very place where the visitor felt herself positioned while experiencing that special swan moment at Loch Nell. Appropriately enough, author's David Carson and Jamie Sams, emphasizing Native American traditions, associate the swan with "altered states of awareness" (p. 193).

As an archetype, the swan is something of a death symbol, but its emphasis is more on spiritual transition and, as Foreman experienced, perfection. In *The Swan of Tuonela*, the famous symphonic tone-poem by Finnish composer Jean Sibelius, the swan passes over death's dark waters. Cirlot defines the swan as one of "the essential symbols of the mystic journey to the other world" (pp. 306, 307). Richard Wagner's Lohengrin is, in fact, a "swan-knight," whose barque is drawn by a swan, actually a human prince. The boy was assumed dead but had actually been transformed into the animal as a special servant to the knights of the Grail, to which Lohengrin belongs. In the final scene of the music-drama, Lohengrin restores the prince to his human guise and kingdom. Here, the swan comes into its true symbolic element, signifying transformation through death to rebirth. In Greek mythology, the sun god's chariot is pulled back across the night sky by a swan.

The animal reappears in another Grail opera, Wagner's last stage work, *Parsifal*, in which the "pure fool" witlessly kills a sacred swan for sport. The enraged knights force Parsifal to observe closely the pathetic death agony of the innocent creature, who only wanted to live and, in so living, brighten the world with its beauty. Moved to tears, with remorse and compassion filling his heart for the first time, he breaks his bow across his knee. The swan dies, but enlightenment is born in the youth. Connecting with Parsifal's growth in sensitivity, Carson and Sams note that the swan is synonymous in Native American thought with "evolving spiritually...the development of the higher mind [and] other levels of awareness" (p. 193).

Second only to birds in synchronous events involving animals are fish. As Cirlot points out, "all symbols are really functions and signs imbued with energy," (pp.101, 102) the fish no less and perhaps especially so. Fish are an obvious archetype of those forces that move through the depths of the subconscious mind. The frequent appearance of fish in the life of psychologist Jung, whose work concerned subconscious phenomena, was entirely proper. The fish theme's timely appearances confirmed certain suspicions he had concerning ongoing research or assisted him by commenting on problems still being resolved in his mind. It was as though, in projecting his conscious and subconscious thoughts on his natural surroundings, the environment was responding to him in a kind of sign language with its most fitting symbol.

On one such occasion, as he himself confessed, "It is, admittedly, exceedingly odd that the fish theme recurs no less than six times within twenty-four hours." These piscine events began in the morning, when he noticed an inscription describing an ancient religious image that was half-man, half-fish. At lunch, he was served fish; then he heard someone mention the Swiss expression of making an "April fish" (a fool) of somebody. In the afternoon, he was shown photographs of fish by a former patient whom he happened to see for the first time in nearly a year. That evening, somebody else showed him an embroidery decorated with the likenesses of fish. The following morning, another patient, absent for ten years, told him of a dream she'd had the night before about a large fish. Months later, having just finished writing down a description of these synchronicities, he saw a large fish lying on the seawall near his home (pp. 10, 11).

Perhaps the most magical animal in the sea and the one closest to humans, at least in a spiritual sense, is the dolphin. It was so sacred to the Greeks that to kill one was a capital offense. Indeed, from ancient times to the present, accounts of strange, wonderful human relationships with dolphins continue to be told, often involving their voluntary rescue of drowning victims.

Their telepathic sense was demonstrated recently in a very meaningful coincidence at a coastal Florida ocean park. A long, narrow channel was dug inland, providing the creatures a direct outlet to the sea, while visitors could get a close view of them in shallow water. One morning, a small crowd of tourists was walking along the banks of the channel, when a single, medium-sized, female dolphin gently tossed a small pebble from the tip of its snout at one of the women visitors. The pebble hit the woman softly on her stomach, to everyone's amusement. They were amazed, however, when the dolphin reappeared to launch another well-aimed pebble at the same woman, striking her harmlessly again on the stomach. Going for a third time, the woman stood facing the edge of the water, waiting for the dolphin's return. A few moments later, it resurfaced and flung yet another tiny stone accurately at the woman's midsection.

"What could have caused it to act so strangely?" wondered the tour director, who had never seen such dolphin behavior before.

"Well," the targeted visitor said, "she knew something no one else but I was aware of. I just learned yesterday that I am pregnant." Appropriately, according to Carson and Sams, among Native Americans, the dolphin is a symbol of "the breath of life,...and breaks the limits and dimensions of physical reality so that we may enter the Dreamtime" (p. 197).

The whale, though encountered less frequently, is a related archetype. Its effective role as a connecting element in synchronicity may be demonstrated by the following meaningful coincidence. With no particular agenda in mind, a photographer, Mike Solarzano, was walking along the beach on the Hawaiian island of Oahu. For about two years, he had been developing an interest in Lemuria, the ancient civilization allegedly responsible for early cultures in both Asia and the Americas before it was lost beneath the Pacific Ocean many thousands of years ago in a series of natural catastrophes. Having learned from the Hawaiians and Canada's Pacific Coast Indians some legends that apparently preserved memories of Lemuria, he was writing a book on the subject and hoped to find something he could photograph that would make a dramatic cover illustration. After a few hours casually wandering along the coast, Mike observed a rugged, offshore island, bare and wave-beaten, which seemed suitable. But too many clouds made the light bad, and tourists kept walking in front of him whenever he tried to shoot. At last, he saw his opportunity and hit the shutter, just once. Given the difficult conditions, he assumed the results would not amount to much.

After developing all his photographs, he came across his lone shot of the offshore island. It was not as bad as he expected, and a tiny anomaly at the edge of the print caught his attention. He thought the almost imperceptible speck, somewhat comma-shaped, must be a mote of dust and wondered if the developer or his camera were at fault. When he examined the supposed imperfection through a magnifying glass, however, he was surprised to see that it was not extraneous dust that had somehow worked its way into the print, but something he'd actually photographed. As he focused in yet closer, his surprise turned to astonishment. There, just barely within the shot, and obviously a great distance out at sea, was a whale lurching out of the water up to its tail, the bulk of its enormous body completely exposed in the air. This dramatic breach is known as a "spy hop," because the animal is believed to use its brief moment in midair to survey its surroundings. During the week Mike spent in Oahu, he never saw so much as a whale's fin.

Mike remembered the unstructured, even indifferent nature of the afternoon of this remarkable shot, made in conscious ignorance. Had he taken it a split second just before or after it broke the surface, the whale would not have been captured on film. But the photographer's sense of wonder at this splendid coincidence shot up to awe when he suddenly remembered a line from Carson and Sams' book, *Medicine Cards: The Discovery of Power Through the Ways of Animals*, on Native American symbols: "In tribal legend, Whale's move into the ocean happened when the Earth shifted and Lemuria, the Motherland, went below the waves" (p. 201). He recalled that he had gone out on the Oahu beach specifically to photograph something to be used as a cover for his proposed book about Lemuria.

Moreover, the whale is also recognized as the Record Keeper, who is supposed to have chronicled all the past events of our planet, underlying the photographer's intention to write a history of the sunken civilization. Whether or not one believes such a place actually existed is immaterial, as regards the synchronicity itself. An acausal connection linking Mike's casual visit at Oahu and his desire to publish a book about Lemuria with the extremely rare appearance of a whale, the Lemurian symbol par excellence, amounted to a mystical set of coincidences, all closely related although beyond the control of any human agency.

An ancient society with its own peculiar coincidence was the pre-Inca Nazca civilization, located in the arid Peruvian desert near the Pacific Coast, south of the capital Lima. Its creators left behind dozens of huge line drawings that they etched into the ground about two thousand years ago. The drawings depict birds, lizards, a spider, and a menagerie of other animals and plants, together with many geometric designs, including trapezoids, lozenges, and spirals. Why they were made is a question still debated by scholars. Although she did not discover them, Maria Reiche arrived in Peru from Germany in the early 1930s and almost immediately became the most important person connected with the Nazca drawings. A professional mathematician, not an archaeologist, she spent the next six decades personally surveying the enigmatic figures, while simultaneously leading a single-handed fight for their preservation. Now that she is blind, bedridden, and in her nineties, her life's work, for which she received scant remuneration, has finally won her international recognition and universal honors in her adopted country.

From the first moment she saw the Nazca designs, she was obsessed with their study. They crowded out all other interests in her life, personal as well as professional. Her whole existence focused into a single purpose, Reiche chose to live alone in a desert hovel at the mercy of bandits and venomous snakes, so she could always be close to the ancient figures. Indifferent to her poverty, she cared only about the time she used—decades, it turned out—to survey the mysterious designs, virtually all that remained of a vanished race. A very close-mouthed woman, she has never publicly discussed the basis for her fanatical devotion to this study, nor has she ever evidenced spiritual inclinations of any kind.

Near the beginning of her survey work at the Nazca Plain, she was carefully measuring a great spiral etched into the desert, when she realized it was part of a much larger design in the image of a monkey; the spiral was only its tail. Months of painstaking work eventually revealed the bioglyph, this enigmatic representation of an animal, in its entirety. But when she completed the outline of the creature's right hand, the last detail to be surveyed, she was startled to see that it was missing its thumb. The left hand showed all five digits. Maria Reiche looked down at her own right hand, which, since birth, was missing a thumb. She said she laughed out loud when she realized the comparison.

Like the fish, the monkey-as-archetype signifies subconscious activity and is credited in some cultures with the ability to grant longevity, success, and protection—all of which typified Reiche's Peruvian experience. But, at least in her case, the symbolism appears to go much deeper. To some esoteric observers, the right-hand thumb missing from both the ancient illustration and the modern surveyor is the clue to her obsessive motivation. They read it as a sign that she is the original, ancient artist reincarnated after two thousand years in the body of Reiche to restore and preserve this work.

On the other side of the world from Peru, not a monkey figure but a dog played a role in an instance of synchronicity that likewise seemed to recall connections to some remote past. During the spring of 1988, vacationing students from Heidelberg University were visiting the Italian ruins of Ostia, long ago the port of Rome. Ostia's large, typically open-air theater is virtually intact, despite the passage of the last twenty centuries, and it was here that the students decided to have some fun. They loudly challenged one of their classmates to go down on the vacant stage in front of all the other tourists from various parts of the world and make a speech in classical Latin.

Embarrassed but urged on by the demanding applause of his friends, the student descended the ancient stone stairway and made his way to the center arena. There he delivered an amusing tirade, tripping over his Latin and lapsing into a rowdy German dialect, much to the guffaws and laughter of not only his fellow classmates, but also the foreign tourists. He wound up the buffoonish oration by blaming his faulty memory on the gods to whom places such as Ostia had been raised and declared he would no longer place any trust in them, unless they showed up here and now. He bowed deeply to his applauding audience, then quit the stage.

As he did so, his spectators suddenly fell into a stunned silence, as they beheld a very large, black, menacing-looking dog, resembling a wolf, its underside hanging with swollen teats, slowly emerge from a wall at the far end of the theater, then walk to the center stage. It stood at precisely the same spot only seconds before occupied by the mocking orator, regarding the spellbound crowd. After a few long moments, the dog passed in a stately, deliberate walk down the center aisle of the theater and out through the front entrance, where it disappeared among the other ruins of Ostia. The students only broke their wide-eyed silence when the clownish speaker voiced in a low tone the thought that must have been on everybody's mind: "That dog looked like the wolf that suckled Romulus and Remus, the founders of Rome!"

In this instance of synchronicity, the dog and wolf symbols interfaced with each other, as recognized by the student's reaction to the animal's dramatic stage entrance. Its identification with the wolf of Rome's foundation legend is apparent enough, but less well known was the wolf's role in ancient myth as the guardian of great monuments, of which the theater at Ostia was one, where sacred, as well as mundane, productions were regularly performed. The wolf was also regarded as a ruler of the land of the dead, or the Otherworld. In Native American tradition, the wolf is associated with the moon, or the psychic side of life, and is known as the Teacher, a role it apparently assumed for the irreverent students.

Dogs being common household pets, stories abound of their often uncanny synchronous behavior and interactions with their human companions. A typical example took place around my dinner table one evening. A friend was telling me that her big husky, Ivan, who was attentively watching her speak, had once devoured a candle. "Would you do that again?" she asked him. I seemed to read either his mind or the expression on his face and spoke for him, saying, "Try me!" Also sitting at the table was another friend, David, previously lost in thought, who suddenly looked up in surprise. He said we had all just participated in a synchronicity that only he recognized. Immediately previous to and during our discussion about Ivan's preference for candles, David was seriously considering a problem his Masonic lodge was having with candles for a second-degree ceremony to be conducted the following evening. Not only that, but at the precise moment I spoke for Ivan, David thought of the ritual response given by an initiate in the candle ceremony, which is, "Try me!"

More often encountered than the wolf and less frequently seen than the dog, the fox is an archetype stranger than both but not unrelated to either. Jung recounted a synchronous meeting with the animal, as he was walking outdoors through a wooded area at the side of a patient. She was in the process of telling him about a dream she'd had when a youngster, in which she saw a ghostly fox coming down the stairs of her parents' home. Just at that moment, a real fox came out of the trees about a hundred feet ahead of them and walked along casually for several minutes. Jung remarked that the animal behaved as though "it were a partner in the situation" (Bolen, p. 20).

Fox symbolism speaks of shape shifting, lycanthropy (woman into fox), and all forms of physical as well as psychic change, most often involving female transcendence. The fox is considered the most magical animal in Japan, where, as Inari, it is the messenger of the harvest god. Among Native Americans, the fox was believed to protect families and keep them together by catering to each immediate relative. Interestingly, all of the foregoing mythic traditions from Europe, Asia, and America directly pertain to Jung's patient. When she had the dream as a girl she was approaching adolescence, which turned out to be a very bountiful period of her life; this recalls Inari as messenger of the harvest god. Her devotion to her paternal family, which was particularly tightknit, was likewise reflected in the domestic emphasis given to the fox by Native Americans. While little of all this was news to the woman, the highly appropriate symbolism focused in such a meaningful coincidence acted to confirm her personal dedication.

An animal encounter that did exert a powerful transformation in another woman's life likewise signaled a turning point in Jung's research, because it forcefully opened him to consideration of synchronicity's profound psychological basis. The story is well known, but deserves to be sketched here, since it is a classic example of modern ostenta with which everyone interested in synchronicity should be familiar.

At a decisive moment in her treatment, a female client was describing a vividly recollected dream, in which someone presented her with a costly piece of jewelry fashioned in the image of a scarab beetle. She was a particularly troublesome case—"psychologically inaccessible," according to Jung—a young person whose strongly narrow view of the world admitted no reality beyond that which was not immediately and physically perceptible and rationally acceptable. Because of her unswerving, materialistic mindset, her treatment had come to an impasse. But as she related her dream of the golden scarab, Jung heard a distinct tapping at the window. He saw that the sound was being made by a large insect that seemed intent on getting inside. Jung opened the window and caught the creature as it flew past him, then gave it to his patient with the words, "Here is your scarab." In her hands she held a scarabaeid beetle, its gold-green color nearly matching the golden scarab jewel of her dream. The dumbfounded woman's exclusively rationalistic world view was severely shaken, so much so that she was at last open to further treatment, which eventually concluded with positive results. The meaningful coincidence had no less a profound effect on Jung himself; it led him to his pioneering investigation of synchronicity. He noted that no beetle had ever before or since made such a racket at his window. In fact, he could not even remember seeing an insect of this kind so late in the season.

An old, central-European, folk belief holds that if a beetle flies into one's house, it is an omen of unexpected news (Leach, p. 212). But in Egyptian mythology, the insect is better known. Scarabs were emblems of Khepera, seen in the morning sun, daily confirmation of his function as the god of resurrection. His name means at once "Scarab" and "He Who Becomes," or "The Becomer" (Mercatante, pp. 83, 84). Living beetles were looked upon as his physical incarnation, so Egyptians wore scarab amulets to attract Khepera's regenerative power. Remarkably, in her dream, Jung's patient was presented with a scarab amulet that, in her waking state, summoned its animal counterpart (or so the ancient Egyptians would have believed). And the meeting of the subconscious symbol with its biological object generated in her a powerful regenerative change for the better, the kind of born-again experience that characterized Khepera, "The Becomer."

Joseph Campbell, who devoted his life to studying Jung's subconscious correlation of myth, experienced his own appropriate synchronicity. Living in New York City at the time, he was intensely studying a book on Bushman mythology, in which the praying mantis plays the hero's role. In the midst of his reading, Campbell felt a sudden urge to open the window. As he did so, he was flabbergasted to see the largest praying mantis he'd ever encountered crawling along the rim. As he studied it more closely, the insect swiveled its head and looked directly at the astonished mythologist. "His face looked just like a Bushman's face," Campbell recalled (Combs and Holland, p. 31). The statistical improbability of this meaningful coincidence was heavily underscored by the apartment's location fourteen floors above 6th Avenue, an unlikely place to find such a large specimen. Interestingly, Campbell's synchronicity bears an uncanny resemblance to that experienced by his predecessor. Jung, too, was greeted by a timely insect at his window, itself an archetype. The window is an aperture to the Otherworld beyond our material plain of existence.

A newspaper reporter was writing about a Hollywood movie producer he'd just described as a "blood-sucking mosquito of a man," when he was buzzed by a large mosquito. The creature did not generate his metaphor, because he had not seen any insects in his room all year till then.

A different sort of insect connected two friends who were otherwise separated by five hundred miles. One of them happened to find hanging from a tree in a neighbor's yard the largest, most ornately designed caterpillar he had ever seen. It belonged to the cecropia moth, the biggest in North America. When he described it to his friend in a long-distance telephone conversation, both were amazed to learn that on the same day and perhaps at the same hour that the caterpillar made its appearance, the other friend had read of the cecropia moth for the first time; until then, he had been ignorant of the insect. The date this coincidence occurred became more meaningful when they realized that it was the anniversary of the death of a mutual friend.

The Bantu believe the souls of the dead take the forms of caterpillars, to be reborn as beautiful moths and butterflies. The same concept prevailed in ancient Rome, from whence derived the very word larva, which meant "ghost" or "spirit" (Leach, p. 185). In this case, the appearance of an extraordinary caterpillar reinforced a higher-minded bond between two friends, however separated by distance, through the tragedy of their fallen comrade. Beyond the spiritual link thus created in a magical event that seemed to transcend death, its symbol spoke of something still incubating inside the larva of time.

We have examined the synchronistic interplay of the bird, fish, monkey, dog, fox, and insect. All the other beasts we might meet with, either in our dreams or waking state, would require a book all their own. One of the best of its kind is Carson and Sams' *Medicine Cards: The Discovery of Power Through the Ways of Animals*, listed in the bibliography of this book. Suffice it here to briefly include a few creatures most commonly known to carry meaningful coincidence into our lives.

The household cat above all personifies grace and the ability to softly pass between opposing forces via the art of serene balance. Its larger relatives—the puma, lion, tiger, leopard, cheetah, and panther—are variations on the themes of leadership, will, single-mindedness, the pride and power of standing apart, and a law unto oneself. Squirrels signify mischief-making, gossip, selfishness—characteristics mythologized in the ancient Norse tales of Ratatoesk, the rumor-mongering squirrel who tried to incite conflict between the gods of Asgaard and the monsters of the underworld.

The bear, because of his deathlike hibernation, is an archetype for the power of reincarnation. Bear-shaped effigy mounds oriented to the sunrise of the winter solstice were sculpted from the earth two thousand years ago by an unknown people on the shores of Devil's Lake, Wisconsin. The first day of winter signaled the beginning of the animal's hibernation season.

The elusive deer symbolizes the transient nature and impermanence of all things. The mouse speaks of scrutiny, the rat of vulgar greed, the rabbit of fear.

The turtle is a complex, but powerful, archetype. It stands for astral projection, the transformation of the soul through various spiritual dimensions—just as the turtle successfully survives on land as well as under the water. The Native American name for North America is Turtle Island, after the arrival of their ancestors following the cataclysmic transformation of the Great Flood, the Great Purging or Cleansing, in which many who turned away from the gods perished. Frog and turtle share the same symbolism. To the Chumash Indians of southern California, Dancing Frog was a shaman whose medicine originated at a time before the Great Flood.

The horse epitomizes either the power of liberty or strength through self-control, depending on the nature of the synchronistic experience. Because it is able to shed its old skin for a new one, the snake represents the ability to regenerate, to outgrow the old and emerge strong and refreshed. Sometimes, like the serpent itself, the process is frightening, but snakes are messengers of fundamental, necessary change for the better.

The foregoing instances of ostenta comprise a tiny fraction of the phenomenon. Almost every animal on Earth has its own symbolism. But the interpretation of these symbols, although assisted by mythic traditions and psychology, depends for its final authority on the person or persons to whom the symbol is presented. Mere lists of such symbols that attempt to offer parallel explanations or meanings are only somewhat helpful. A snake might be an object of horror for one person and signify something entirely positive for someone else. All-inclusive explanations for personal symbols, however fundamentally universal they may be, are of little value. The foregoing interpretations of specific cases do not comprise any standard against which all other actual events must be deciphered. Instead, they are described in order to demonstrate how each instance of synchronicity may be approached by following common or archetypal themes and their effects on the people who experience them.

Noting these meaningful animal coincidences might lead us to ask if synchronicity is confined to human experience or takes place among all creatures. Apparently acausal events occur ceaselessly throughout the animal kingdom. Pet owners report numerous synchronicities not only between themselves and their charges, but among the animals themselves. We humans are perhaps unique only in that we consciously recognize such events and endeavor to understand them. Actually, the other creatures of the planet may be far more advanced than we are in the appreciation of synchronicity, because they act upon it instinctually and their behavior is conditioned by it.

The examples cited here demonstrate how synchronicity can connect the activities of human beings with apparently unrelated meteorologic and geologic events, as well as with animal behavior. We are surrounded by a universe of active symbols whose relevance extends beyond our generalizations. Yet, these symbols often appear tailored to our individual situations and enlightenment. It is that deeply personal, even intimate, connection with a guiding reality beyond our five senses that we experience through the magical moments of synchronicity we encounter in the natural world.

chapter**3**

The Synchronicity
of Prophesy

*The Future casts its shadow before itself, but we more
often shudder half-knowing in the whiff of its throw than
actually see the complete outline of its silhouette.*
—Johann-Wolfgang von Goethe, *The West-Eastern Divan*

Some synchronicities seem to predict coming events. Similar to
incidents of this kind are those that take place at the same time but
are so widely separated in space they defy any rational explanations. The factor they all seem to share is an altered state of
consciousness experienced by the people involved in them. The
synchronicities described in the following sections generally occur
at moments during which the mind has less direct control over its
surroundings, when the fully alert waking state has surrendered to
subconscious influences. Dreams, wherein these influences
dominate completely, represent the most obvious psychological
staging areas for precognitive episodes.

Being in love is a waking altered state of awareness that, because of its profound, sometimes obsessive nature, often interfaces with dreams. So too, some of the most credible examples of telepathy have been unlooked-for events, in which the unknowing participants were not deliberately focused on establishing any mind-to-mind connections. Premonitions usually begin emotionally, as some nameless feeling that eventually finds expression as the feeling becomes more powerful. Such events may be brought about through an altered consciousness by way of visual stimuli in the form of archetypal images, as depicted in the mandalas of Tibetan Buddhism or the tarot card deck.

Whatever the method or related category of synchronicity, the numerous instances of human experience they encompass force us to reconsider our commonly held notions, long taken for granted, about the nature of time. Of more direct bearing on our investigation of meaningful coincidence, they appear to demonstrate that even (or especially) in our subconscious mind we are individually, however subtly, connected to the Great Enigma.

Premonition

Premonition is awareness of an action before it takes place. Of all the categories of synchronicity, it is perhaps the most elusive. Coming events may cast their own shadows, as the common saying goes, but belief in the foreknowledge of their arrival has become confused by the conclusion of most psychologists, who believe that such incidents are actually the inevitable outcome of wish fulfillment.

A man in my survey, Earl Koenig, said he always laid out a lengthy spread of tarot cards before he planned an overseas trip. The tarot originated as a game in early fourteenth-century Italy, but even then it incorporated much older alchemical symbols used for divination. Before one of his trips, Koenig's reading of the cards told him he would have a most productive and enjoyable journey, except that he would, sometime in the course of his travels, experience a poignant sense of loss. Wanting to learn more, he pulled additional cards, which indicated that, while the experience would not be at all life-threatening or even particularly important, he would nevertheless feel a momentary sting of remorse while in the Canary Islands because of some missing object. A final reading reassured him that he should go on his trip. For the next three months, Earl traveled throughout Europe and North Africa enjoying himself, as was predicted. By the time he reached the island of Tenerife, in the Canaries, he had entirely forgotten the card reading, but it was there that he misplaced a precious gift he'd received from a friend while visiting in Slovenia. Only in the midst of his deep disappointment over the lost item did he recall the prediction of the tarot, months earlier, back in the States.

The Dream State

Some of the most extraordinary, although less frequent, examples of synchronicity occur in dreams. The possibility that the event represents merely wish fulfillment can be ruled out, together with any deliberate or subconscious actions on the part of the person or people involved. The sleep state represents a pure field of action uncontaminated by extraneous influences, where acausality can play itself out freely. Synchronicity in dreams seems especially powerful, because we have absolutely no control over the circumstances and are entirely in the grip of an ordering, connecting mystery that has included us in its design. Dreams of future developments that sometimes come to pass may be only our subconscious mind sorting out known problems in the relaxed objectivity of sleep. But those dreams that accurately prefigure events absolutely separate from and unknown to the sleeper arise from other sources less rationally traced to their origins.

An outstanding case in point is Edgar Cayce, an uneducated, good-hearted man who lived in rural Kentucky and then Virginia in the late nineteenth century. Cayce is still remembered as the Sleeping Prophet for his visions of the future while in an induced trance state. His waking interests did not extend much beyond his family and the Bible. But while sleeping, he made remarkable statements about medical cures, geology, archaeology, and even spirituality that were often at odds with his fundamentalist Christian upbringing. Although he never recalled his utterances, more than 14,000 were recorded until his death in 1945. Some dealt with future events that have since come to pass.

Among the most outstanding examples concerned a Chicago woman who wrote to him in desperation in the mid-1920s about an exceptionally painful rash that covered much of her body. Years of treatment by leading physicians had failed to cure her condition or determine its cause. Drifting into his dream consciousness, Cayce said that the source of her ailment would be found shortly after she received his written response; indeed, after she received his letter she found the nest of a poisonous recluse spider that, unbeknownst to her, had bitten her. The ointment Cayce prescribed put her rash into remission.

A few months later, Cayce said that scientists would someday learn that thousands of years ago a major, now vanished, tributary of the Nile River flowed across what is now the Sahara Desert from the Egyptian Delta to the Atlantic Ocean on the other side of North Africa in present-day Morocco. At the time he made this prediction, in the early 1930s, geologists universally regarded his statement as nothing less than imaginative fantasy. Yet, sixty years later, during a satellite-mapping project of the North African Desert undertaken as part of a joint European-U.S. space program in 1991, Landsat instruments displayed the clearly defined riverbed of an enormous waterway snaking its way from the Nile Delta across the vastness of the Sahara to end near the Atlantic coastal city of Mogadir in southern Morocco. What seemed utterly beyond the realm of possibility to the scientific world of his day had been revealed to Edgar Cayce while he slept.

Cayce was unique only in the great number of prescient dreams he experienced. Such exceptional psychodramas, as Jung designated them, occur to many people, less frequently, but no less profoundly.

Precognitive Dreams

A person who experiences a precognitive dream perceives an event or condition before it takes place. Such dreams do not always connect with traumatic situations, but the more dramatic ones are usually better recollected. As an example of a less compelling sleeping prophecy, Adrian Rhinehart, a professional driver, told me he has had several predictive dreams, all concerning his demanding occupation. The events predicted in the dreams came to pass just as he remembered them from the dreams and always involved traffic accidents, although no one was ever injured or died in any of them. Rhinehart related a vivid dream in which he was driving down an unfamiliar road, when he looked ahead to see a car turned upside-down near the gutter. He slowed as he approached the scene, where a solitary policeman waved him on. Later that day, he did indeed find himself driving on a street he'd never seen before and came to a vehicle resting on its roof, precisely as in the dream. There was even a lone traffic cop motioning him forward. The driver said he took such dreams very seriously and claimed they expanded his awareness, however subtly, thereby helping him to avoid accidents.

But Rhinehart had not paid these dreams much attention until one night when he dreamt that he was driving over a bridge and lost control of his car. As it broke through a guardrail, he jumped out the door but grabbed the seat belt. Secured safely on the bridge, he held his car suspended from its seat belt for as long as he could, until he had to let go, and the vehicle fell about a hundred feet into the sea, where it vanished. He awoke from the dream thinking, "I'm going to total my car today!" But after he was fully awake, he shrugged off the dream as so much nonsense and went to work without a care. That afternoon, he fell asleep at the wheel while driving over a bridge and collided with the rear end of the car in front of him. Although no one was hurt, the damage to his own vehicle was extensive. Even so, he believed, against reason, that it could be fully repaired. Only after two or three days did he reluctantly admit it was a total wreck.

"No one can tell me I was the victim of my own wish fulfillment," he insisted. "That was my favorite car and my livelihood, which I enjoyed, depended on. Others may choose to believe I subconsciously destroyed my own vehicle just to make a dream come true, but I know in my heart they are patently incorrect."

Interestingly, both accidents—the one in the dream and the other on the road—took place when he was asleep. In the dream, he held on to the seat belt until he eventually had to let go, losing his car to oblivion; so too, after crashing his vehicle in public, he could not admit the obvious, that the car was totaled, until long after the accident itself. In other words, he refused to let go of his car.

A precognitive dream experienced by Julie Westmar, an Oregon woman, utterly ruled out any possibility of wish fulfillment. She dreamt she was inside a two-story building, distinct but unknown, with seven strangers after dark. Everyone was frightened because the place was surrounded by a pack of lions wielding firearms. But the lions were eventually dispersed by an eighth stranger who arrived at the building. Westmar repeated this absurd dream to her husband. He was amazed several days later when, while visiting Seattle, they recognized the very building she'd described. They had to go inside the building to meet a sociologist friend, with whom they shared the remarkable coincidence. He asked Westmar if anyone had been hurt in her dream, then led them to a window and pointed out a developing situation on the streets below. Their building was surrounded by a teenage gang, whose members wore T-shirts clearly emblazoned with the name Lions. Afraid, the sociologist turned off the lights inside the building. Now he and his friends could see that the criminals were openly brandishing handguns. He noticed that there were seven people, most of them unknown to one another, waiting fearfully in the room together. Shortly thereafter, the sociologist's wife arrived, saw the gang members, and telephoned the police, who dispersed the Lions. She was the eighth person on the scene (Ryback and Sweitzer, pp. 131, 132).

A majority of precognitive dreams concern death or life-threatening situations. People who claim to dream about airline disasters in advance of an actual crash receive publicity from time to time. To put such claims to the test, I arranged for a close friend, Jim Harris, who said he experienced such dreams to contact me immediately after he had one. Not many months passed before Harris telephoned to describe a dream in which a small, single-engined private plane was erratically climbing and descending, then climbing again, as though its pilot were desperately searching for something. With a frightening maneuver, the aircraft suddenly struck the ground, killing everyone aboard. Harris remembered the plane lying on one side, its wing in the air at an awkward angle, the white fuselage designed with red trim and numbering. The crashed plane lay in an area surrounded by trees.

There were no reports of any downed aircraft the next morning or afternoon. But later that night, the news showed the crumpled remains of a civilian plane that had come down in a local park after nightfall. Television coverage revealed that the aircraft lay on one side with a wing angled into the air. Its white fuselage was clearly marked with red trim and identification numbers. It seems the pilot, its lone occupant, died in the accident after becoming lost and disoriented in heavy clouds, which he alternately tried to climb over or dive beneath, until he struck the ground, which, apparently, he saw just before pulling up too late. Jim's dream of the crash, some thirty-six hours before it happened, matched the actual event point for point.

This dream, like the others, distressed him, primarily because his dreams never included enough information for him to change the outcome in waking life. For all their often exact details, they always lacked a specific number or some other feature by which he could identify the doomed aircraft. These disastrous visions lasted over a period of about seven years, from his late twenties into his mid-thirties. He averaged three to five per year. When they no longer came to him, Jim did not regret their absence. On the contrary, he felt relieved from the unhappy stress of knowing that an impending catastrophe was beyond his control to prevent. Why he had been given these series of precognitive dreams he never understood. But as to their veracity, he has never had any doubt.

Although most precognitive dreams appear to be concerned with life-and-death issues, they are not all as negative or frustrating as Harris's dreams of disaster. Timothy Gray and Alex Tanous cite the case of a woman who was plagued with migraines. Doses of codeine gave her only partial relief. One night, she dreamt that her body was attached by wires to a small, mysterious box of some kind, which she referred to in her dream as "the battery pack of life." Six months later, her physician offered her a neurotransmitter, a small, battery-powered device that sent electrical impulses to the brain, thereby short-circuiting its sensitivity to pain just as the migraines began.

Until she saw the neurotransmitter, she had completely forgotten her dream, wherein she had precisely envisioned this medical apparatus. Over the next two years, it mitigated the worst effects of her headaches and made her consider a holistic approach to health, including meditation. She believes that "the battery pack of life" prompted her to embrace the alternative methods that led to the subsequent improvement of her condition (Gray and Tanous, pp. 22, 23).

Shared Dreams

We move even farther afield from explanations of wish fulfillment in the synchronous phenomenon of shared, mutual, or simultaneous dreams. Here, two individuals participate at the same time in a subconscious psychodrama common to both. These dreams usually occur between people who are intellectually or emotionally close and, at least in some instances, suggest the operation of telepathy while the mind is not focused on conscious activity. Steven Francis and Richard Kazume, two friends in my survey group, have documented a number of dreams in which they appeared together simultaneously, despite the fact that one of them had moved out of the state to a location several hundred miles away. In one such example, they both dreamt that they were in attendance at the same public meeting of a famous political statesman who'd actually died years before they were born. Interestingly, details of both dreams revealed that, while both dreamers were at the same event, each had a different point of view, as though standing in different places among the crowd.

A few months later, Kazume, the younger of the two, dreamt of a kind of metal pillbox. It was a rounded, metal enclosure with a sparse interior, military in nature and located either near or on water. That same night, unbeknownst to the dreamer, his friend had been staying up late reading about the *Monitor*, a famous Union ironclad ship of the American Civil War. The vessel was unique for its large, metal turret, which contained nothing more than a pair of cannons. While not a shared dream, this synchronicity demonstrates how the thoughts of one person may penetrate the subconscious of another, even without conscious volition.

A single dream in which three people simultaneously participated included a woman, her mother, and her best friend. It centered on a young, unidentified pregnant girl. They all shared the same dream and amazed one another when they discussed its familiar details. Each one of them remembered the dream as particularly vivid, save for the identity of the pregnant girl. The three dreamers could not imagine who the child might be. Several days later, the woman was taken into confidence by her fourteen-year-old sister, who had just learned that she was pregnant. Until then, no one had suspected the girl might be pregnant. The shared dream had taken place the same night the girl was made aware of her condition (Ryback, p. 59). It appears that the mechanism for this triple synchronicity was the affection all three women felt for the young girl. In this example, our categories merge to include prescient dreaming with the power of love, described later in this chapter. Often, when people are closely linked, either through blood ties or emotional bonding, major disruptions in their relationship appear to generate poignant instances of synchronicity.

Although telepathy seems to have been the common denominator of these shared dreams, skeptics who reject the credibility of this phenomenon are left with alternatives far more difficult for them to consider, chief among them being the possibility of an equally unseen but no less determining power linking otherwise separate individuals through common events. People intolerant of explanations beyond any standard rational interpretation reject out of hand suggestions for a spiritual cause. But in so doing, they miss the opportunity of having their cake and eating it, too, because telepathy, while a veritable phenomenon, is itself an expression of synchronicity, as the following section demonstrates.

Telepathy

The word telepathy derives from the Greek *tele*, meaning far off, and *pathein*, which means to sense, feel, or perceive. It defines direct communication through the transmission of thoughts, or thought transference, as the Theosophists describe, from one human mind to another mind or several other minds. Although telepathy is nonvisual, it is occasionally accompanied by sounds or voices. More often, communication is not auditory but perceived or inwardly sensed.

While any communication between minds through some means other than sensory perception is a useful definition of telepathy, in synchronous events it occurs without the deliberate effort to enter another's thoughts. Although a subconscious telepathic link seems to explain these events, closer examination sometimes suggests that telepathy may be only one of several elements working together to bring off synchronicity. Like precognition, involuntary telepathy often appears to be activated by life-threatening situations.

A scuba diver in Wisconsin, Lloyd Weaver, had just completed a satisfying afternoon of prolonged dives with his friends in a beautiful lake. After they went home, he lingered alone in a park near the shore, where he ate a good lunch. The water and exercise had left him stimulated but relaxed, and he took time to enjoy the perfect late-spring weather. A few children playing in the park added to its idyllic setting, and he lay peacefully at the base of a tree to look out across the blue waters he had earlier enjoyed so thoroughly. He felt perfectly centered, with hardly a thought in his stilled mind. He began to doze off, when an unpleasant memory seemed to surface of its own accord in his thoughts. Weaver unaccountably found himself remembering a friend who had lost his right hand in a factory accident. When he had visited him at the hospital, his friend complained of the pain he felt at the wrist, where the hand had been amputated. He had not thought of his poor friend in twenty years. Why had this memory come back now, in the midst of such a happy day?

Uneasy now, he glanced at his watch—it was precisely 3:23 P.M.—and felt a strong urge to return home as quickly as possible. As soon as he entered his house, he asked his mother if anything was wrong. She told him that his sister, who lived in southern Illinois, nearly five hundred miles away, had fallen and severely injured her wrist. She was in great pain and required extensive medical treatment to save her right hand. The accident, he was informed, had occurred some minutes before 3:30 that same afternoon.

Later, separating the various elements of his synchronicity, Weaver concluded that, although his mind had received the telepathic message of his sister's pain, his subconscious had not been able to break through to his consciousness. It therefore urgently searched his stored lifetime recollections for the nearest comparable memory, which it used forcefully like a mental battering ram to break through to his rational mind and activate his intuitive sense. Weaver also believes that telepathy developed as part of our universal human evolution, when our ancestors hundreds of thousands of years ago lived out among all the dangers of the natural world. Over the course of innumerable generations, our ancestors became highly sensitive to every nuance in a threatening environment. Telepathic intuition was only one of the evolutionary defenses that helped to protect them from trouble. It developed first among immediate family members, who most depended on each other for support, then throughout the tribe or clan. With the advent of cities, wherein walls and armies took over mutual protection, such telepathic senses grew less necessary and atrophied, although they were not completely lost, even after five thousand years of civilization.

At the same lake, Weaver experienced another family synchronicity he deemed essentially telepathic. The previous winter, he had driven out onto the lake's surface of thick ice in his new car. Originally, he had had no intention of doing such a thing, but through a sudden, adventurous impulse, he sped across the frozen water just for fun. Parking in the very middle of the lake, he got out to photograph the car. Not long after, he was seized by a terrible vision of the ice opening up and his new hatchback suddenly crashing front-forward through the broken surface into the depths of the dark water below. Jumping back into the car, he drove it at high speed off the lake and safely onto the shore.

Returning home, he was surprised when his mother asked him if he had been foolish enough to drive his car out on the ice. She told him that her concentration on a crossword puzzle had been suddenly interrupted by a brief vision that flitted across her otherwise occupied thoughts. For hardly more than an instant, she distinctly had the mental impression of his car plunging through the surface into the lake. She experienced the vision around 1:30 P.M., just about the time he felt strongly urged to get off the ice.

Strangely, while both he and his mother clearly envisioned the car disappearing into the water at the same time, he saw it crashing front-forward, while she had it sinking rearward. Such a discrepancy often occurs in instances of telepathy. In a conscious effort at thought transference, I once concentrated on the illustration of a machine gun I had just drawn on a sheet of paper. Although the person to whom I was willing this image said he "got something," he could not identify it. When handed a pencil and paper, he drew the object he saw in his mind's eye, but he was still unable to recognize it until I turned his drawing around; he had drawn the machine gun upside-down. This twisting of otherwise accurately received images, although not understood, is regarded by parapsychologists as a hallmark of authentic thought transference. Similarly, when an image is picked up by a television camera, the same kind of inversion takes place, and a corrective lens is required to set the image rightside up.

Sometimes, synchronous instances of apparently involuntary telepathy connect with seemingly innocuous events. In 1959, a woman washing dishes in her suburban Chicago home began casually thinking of the *Dinah Shore Show*. Those were the days of live TV, when telecasts required intensive rehearsing schedules. The housewife found herself making up skits, numbers, and ensembles for the popular television program to pass the time spent among her pots and pans. Watching the show four or five days later, she was astonished to see it following the same agenda she'd presumed she had invented, virtually detail for detail, down to the identical songs. A few days later, standing over her sink while engaged in the same dreary task, her thoughts almost indifferently drifted to the show again, and the housewife found herself mentally choreographing dance numbers and rehearsing songs. Especially curious to learn if reality could at least once more catch up with her imagination or intuition, she eagerly turned on her television at the scheduled hour. As before, the show was almost exactly the same as her precognitive vision. For the next several weeks, she predicted with incredible accuracy each show days in advance for her newly entertained husband and children. The visions continued for about a month and a half, then ceased altogether, never to return.

Dinah Shore was not the woman's favorite entertainer. Nor did there appear to be any fundamental connection between an unknown Midwestern housewife and the famous California performer. The woman felt her mind had been receiving mental images of someone closely connected with the show's production. Both people were apparently thinking on the same telepathic frequency, at least for around forty-five days. Even though the coincidences left her feeling no closer to Dinah Shore, they did cause her to be more open to accept her own paranormal potential. As a member of our study group, the housewife confessed to a calm sense of purpose she felt after sharing her experiences with others.

In many cases of genuine telepathy, background synchronicities play even subtler roles. Yet, these less obvious undercurrents appear to be the real leading motif of telepathy, just as other meaningful coincidences use different means of connecting humans with synchronous events. The second instance of synchronicity experienced by the scuba diver occurred at a time when he had been somewhat estranged from his sister; his telepathic intuition of her accident and his concern for her health over the ensuing months brought them together again. And although he had always been close to his mother, the simultaneous vision he shared with her of his car breaking through the ice reinforced their closeness.

Love appears to be the universal cause behind many of these supposedly acausal episodes. Many people believe that love in its many forms is the fundamental principle that sets in motion all synchronicity. Indeed, there are enough instances of human affection, with their specific qualities, to merit their own classification. The following case exemplifies the universality of love supposedly underlying other forms of meaningful coincidence and bridges the previously discussed precognitive dream category. It concerns Doris Carlson, a woman from California, who was informed by a psychic reader that she would someday meet a man known as Father John, who would be very close to her. Ten days later, the woman was dancing with a man she'd just met at a New Year's Eve party. The man told her about a new friend he had brought along. The fellow was very shy because of his blindness. He asked if she would mind dancing with him anyway, for just a few minutes. She was surprised he had asked her; of all people at the party she was probably the most willing to accept, because her own mother was blind. After she asked the stranger to join her in a waltz, he rose from his seat and laughingly introduced himself as "Ole' Father John," who could not be expected to dance very well. They fell deeply in love and lived happily ever after as husband and wife (Vaughn, p. 55).

The psychic's precognition was the identifying element that made sense of the others following in a series of coincidences. The love and compassion she had long felt for her mother extended to the man who became her husband, even though she did not seek out someone similarly disabled. Then there is the special significance of the time they met—New Year's Eve—a major transitional time signifying new beginnings.

In another story, from the mid-1940s, a framed sign hung in a shop window indicating the one day of the week a grocery store in Portsmouth, England, would be closed. Two weeks before the owner's son was to be married, the frame was removed for the first time in more than twenty years. Surprisingly, the owner found that a large photograph had been used as backing for the sign. Its faded image showed the proprietor holding a small girl in his arms. The child was recognized as none other than the soon-to-be daughter-in-law of the very man in the old picture. No one was able to explain how it had gotten behind the posted sign or the circumstances of the photograph, since the families of the proprietor and the girl were not known to each other at the time it was taken. In a related coincidence, the name of the little girl who grew up to marry the store owner's son was the same as his daughter's first name, while her husband's Christian name was the same as that of proprietor's son (Vaughn, pp. 54, 55).

In a somewhat similar case, an eight-year-old girl, Helen Montgomery, was playing hide-and-seek in a London park when she found eight shillings and sixpence under loose earth. It seemed a wonderful treasure, and she was allowed to keep it. Much later, as a grown woman, she happened to be strolling with her boyfriend through the same park, when the couple passed the spot where she had excavated the coins nearly thirteen years before. When she told him of her childhood discovery there, he confessed that, as a boy, he had buried the money because he stole it from his mother and was afraid he would get in trouble if he kept it on his person. Returning to dig it up, he realized someone had found his ill-gotten gains. Only after his sweetheart told him her story did both realize that they shared a memorable childhood incident (Stickney, p. 36).

Even after love has long gone, meaningful coincidences may still make connections with past affairs of the heart, perhaps as some kind of solace that they somehow had to be, despite their unhappy endings. An American tourist, Robert Stevens, who had fallen deeply in love with an Irish girl named Iris, was emotionally reeling from their breakup less than a year later when, in a serious effort to forget her, he traveled to Austria. But even amid the cultural greatness and natural beauties of this extraordinary country, he could not stop thinking about her. Late one night, alone and strolling through the deserted streets of Linz, he was wondering how she was doing, when he turned a corner and suddenly saw before him an old stone wall, across which someone had painted the words, "Iris is all right." Remarkably, the statement was written in English.

The incident struck his already susceptible, still distraught state of mind with a profound effect. At first unsure what to make of this confrontation with the unexpected, he rolled the synchronicity around in his mind for the next several days. To be sure, he thought of little else. But eventually a rational, somewhat melancholy resignation settled into his soul, calming his emotions. Regarding his lost Iris with neither bitterness nor regret, he successfully integrated her memory into the history of his life, and he was able to move on.

Enigmas

The various categories of synchronous events provide us with specific definitions that help us understand this elusive phenomenon. But there are maverick instances of meaningful coincidence that refuse to be pigeonholed. They belong to no group of similar incidents and are synchronicities unto themselves. Even so, they merit a classification all their own because of their very singularity. They are enigmas of the first order that share nothing in common with other examples, save that they too are acausal. They feel very meaningful to those who experience them, but they lie beyond our understanding. I call this group the enigma category.

Our final example from the last section leads to the enigma category, because the sad lover, while feeling the mystical power of a synchronous connection, was unable to determine its ultimate significance. Indeed, many coincidences defy all attempts at making any sense of them. But it is because of their very power or the feeling of purpose they instill that they merit their own classification. Sometimes, in their senselessness, they are positively amusing. Among preliterate peoples, meaningful coincidences were associated with the mythic trickster or sacred clown, who personifies the anomalous wrinkle in an otherwise comprehensible universe.

David Goodwin, a member of my research group, was the victim of the trickster late one night when he was stacking books in a home he shared with others. They were fast asleep, so he was careful to keep the big volumes from falling over and awakening his housemates. But somehow the stacks got away from him and started to tumble to the floor, despite his furious efforts to halt the avalanche of literature. As they were crashing about, he was able to randomly grab a single book before all the others collapsed with a terrible racket. He was mortified to see that its cover was illustrated with the painting of a woman urging silence by putting her forefinger to her lips.

Literature played its part in another enigmatic piece of synchronicity. A man driving home one evening was listening to the radio, which was broadcasting information about a forthcoming dramatization of "Never Bet the Devil Your Head," originally a short story by Edgar Allan Poe and one of the great writer's rare attempts at humor. Poe was among the driver's favorite authors. Almost immediately thereafter, a speeding jalopy passed on the left. Its license plate read simply, "POE." The first driver laughed to himself but had no idea what the universe was trying to tell him.

As we observed in the beginning of our investigation, talking license plates are elements in the story of synchronicity. So are printed or painted signs of all kinds, and automobiles are the most accessible vehicles for encountering them. Another driver listening to the radio was outraged at learning from a news broadcast of some piece of recent federal legislation that particularly irked him, so much so that he could not help from exclaiming aloud, "Insane!"

At that very moment, he turned to see the single word "Insane!" spray-painted on a wall flashing by on the expressway. Was somebody confirming his political opinions?

A messenger was at his company dispatch office complaining to fellow workers that a former client who used to give them a great deal of business had not used them for the last several months. No one had heard a word from their once-valued customer. The messenger no sooner made his observation than a call came in from the very client he was discussing.

A reporter for the U.S. Navy was worrying about the completion of an important assignment by the deadline set by his superior officers. He was having trouble writing a submission for a commemorative volume entitled *From Sea to Shining Sea*. Driving a thousand miles from his base for other, unrelated duties and fretting over the little time left before his work was due, he happened to glance at the marquee outside a small church, as he sped by. It read, "From Sea to Shining Sea." He did not know what to make of the coincidence, although he was able to submit his finished report just under the deadline.

Parapsychologist Allan Vaughn recounted that he was once hitchhiking when the first car that approached picked him up. It was driven by a woman named Mrs. Allan who lived on Vaughn Road. She had attended his lecture on synchronicity the night before and was now headed for the same hotel he wanted to reach (Vaughn, p. 26).

While events such as these appear to have little or no comprehensible significance, they nevertheless touch their recipients with the same kind of awe more readily understood synchronicities stir in their beneficiaries. Usually, people on the receiving end of acausal enigmas regard them as confirmations of whatever it is they are engaged in at the time. Since every synchronicity is uniquely personal, outside observers are unable to determine if this conclusion is always correct. Often, however, a singular coincidence that seems meaningless when isolated from those that come before and after it begins to make sense when seen in the context of similar experiences. It can then be regarded as but one piece in a larger mosaic, which, being fitted together with other fragments and viewed from the proper perspective, forms an objective, intelligible picture of one's life experience.

chapter **4**

Our Synchronistic Origins and Baffling Parallel Lives

*Do we see in these singular coincidences the purpose of a
supernatural power to enforce the attention of mankind
to the fact that there is something more in this world than
mere matter?*
— Ignatius Donnelly, diary entry for July 4, 1881

Our origins are the roots of our destiny. And they fundamentally represent our sense of who we are and from whence we came. Therefore, it is not surprising that synchronicity embraces us in often poignant experiences that connect us to places from which we sprang or people who nurtured us from our beginnings. Meaningful coincidences linking us to our spiritual or genealogical primordium deepen feelings of identity and belonging and a sense of place, so important to humans.

Occasionally, these profoundly personal synchronicities reveal one of the most surprising and mysterious aspects of this already enigmatic phenomenon—parallel lives. From ancient times to the present, individual cases of extraordinary coincidences have been reported in which unrelated people, often strangers, shared incredibly multitudinous similarities that no theory of probability could explain. Sometimes the individuals cojoined in unaccountable similitude were separated by great distances, widely divergent cultural backgrounds, or even death. Acausal incidents that establish dramatic contact with individual origins or sometimes unmask a parallel life spring from the same region of meaningful coincidence—namely, the sources of our identity.

Origins

Synchronous events that define or emphasize human roots invariably impart a deepened sense of individuality and oneness to the people who experience them, because they powerfully connect to our racial, national, ancestral, or geographic origins. A typical case involved an American of Irish background whose meaningful coincidences on one Saint Patrick's Day began when he found himself inadvertently writing in his diary with green ink, precisely four months to the day since he'd last used that pen. His personal journal for March 17 reported that he sent a letter to a friend, Rosemary Ellen Guiley, living out of state; that evening, he met a woman who introduced herself as Ellen McGuiley. In the morning, he turned on the radio to hear the great Irish actor Cyril Cusack reading William Butler Yeats's *The Lake at Innisfree*—not an unusual occurrence, considering what day it was—except that, immediately afterward, when he randomly selected a tape from his collection of more than five hundred unmarked cassettes and inserted it into the tape player, he was surprised to hear the same poem again recited by Cusack.

In 1968, Wayne May, today the publisher of *Ancient American*, a national archaeology magazine, became interested in genealogy after his aunt told him that his family tree, with roots in pre-Revolutionary War America, sprouted first in Pennsylvania. He knew no one out east, but, more on a lark than on behalf of any serious research, Wayne and a friend drove cross-country to the Keystone

State. Once there, Wayne found a local telephone book in which he was startled to see three full pages of people named May. "Where do I start?" he wondered. Just for fun, his companion told him to close his eyes, turn around three times, then blindly point to any page. Having faithfully followed these instructions, Wayne called the randomly selected number. A woman's voice came on the line, and he sheepishly told her about his quest.

Surprisingly, she invited him to her home. Mrs. May turned out to be a friendly, middle-aged woman who had little personal interest in genealogy, but she directed him to her son, David H. May, who was fascinated by it. When they met, Wayne was flabbergasted to learn that he and David belonged to the same family. They were just a single generation apart. David confessed that his greatest genealogic frustration had been his failure to learn the names of his great-grandfather's brothers, who served in the Civil War. He had a mid-nineteenth-century photograph of Woodford Clark May, but little more. Providentially, Wayne filled in the sketchy research by not only supplying the names of all six brothers but their photos as well. And David gave Wayne enough data to reconstruct four previous generations of his family tree, information he could have obtained from no one else.

Sometimes, synchronicity involving origins can affect the life and death of a whole civilization. By the early sixteenth century, the Aztecs ruled supreme over most of Mexico. An important part of their religious beliefs centered around the mysterious figure of Quetzalcoatl, the Feathered Serpent. Quetzalcoatl was said to have been a white-skinned, yellow-bearded hero wearing a shiny metal helmet. He and his troop of wise followers arrived over the Atlantic Ocean in the distant past to establish civilization in Middle America. They taught the natives about agriculture, astronomy, architecture, writing, and everything necessary to build a sophisticated society. He was beloved by the people for his wisdom and gentleness; they wept when he sailed away, promising to either return himself one day or send one of his personal emissaries.

Subsequently, the Aztec astronomer-priests determined the precise date of Quetzalcoatl's return, which, they believed, would take place in February 1519, when he would reestablish his reign. Every Aztec emperor since Quetzalcoatl's departure was regarded as a caretaker of society, preserving it for the enigmatic founding father or his ambassador to assume its original ownership.

Exactly as predicted, a bearded white man wearing a steel helmet and in command of similarly accoutered followers arrived in the long-predicted month and year at the Bay of Mexico. He even landed at the same shore, near Veracruz, established by tradition as the place where Quetzalcoatl first stepped ashore in the distant past. The precise opposite of any gentle culture bearer, Hernán Cortés utterly destroyed the Aztec Empire in the name of Spanish Christendom. That he was able to so thoroughly overthrow the dominant power in Middle America, an empire of millions, beginning with only four hundred conquistadors in less than two years' time was possible only because of the meaningful coincidence connecting the historical Cortés to the mythical Feathered Serpent. Since the Spaniards were far more interested in Aztec gold than mythology, they did not realize until after the conquest, somewhat to their amusement, that Cortés had been confused with Quetzalcoatl.

Certainly a most extraordinary case of genealogic synchronicity occurred in March 1997, in a small town in northern Britain. Archaeologists there excavated the well-preserved skeleton of a man they confidently carbon-dated to nine thousand years ago. The remains were in such exceptionally good condition that forensic anthropologists at the local university were able to remove enough DNA material for comparisons with people currently living in the same area of the discovery. The scientists were curious to learn if any genetic similarities might be found between modern residents and the ancient stranger. Six people were chosen for their long family histories (the oldest going back to the eleventh century), one of them a professor at the school where the remains were being examined.

When tested, the other five evidenced some general similarities to the nine-thousand-year-old man, but comparison of the forty-year-old professor's genetic blueprint with that of the excavated skeleton shocked the investigators, himself most of all. Their analysis showed unequivocally that the two sets of DNA matched, proving that he not only belonged to the same family, but was actually the direct linear descendant of the prehistoric British inhabitant buried ninety centuries ago! "I cannot describe to you the emotion that electrifies me whenever I gaze into that skull visage," he said, "and realize that I am looking at the remains of my direct ancestor" ("England's Oldest Man," p. 5).

Parallel Lives

Among the rarest forms that synchronicity takes, parallel lives are perhaps the most inexplicable. I encountered a particularly interesting example of this bizarre synchronous phenomenon in 1996, while engaged in collecting material for this book.

The music coming from the radio was unmistakably Mozart. Although his later symphonies are known well enough, the piece being broadcast by a local fine arts radio station was unfamiliar to me, so I assumed it belonged to an earlier period in his career. Since the compact disc revolution of recent years, many otherwise obscure compositions are being reborn. Forgotten or seldom performed works by masters of the past are now available to a worldwide audience of audiophiles born generations after the composers went to that great concert hall in the sky. I naturally assumed that the sublime music filling my apartment was among the lost or infrequently heard creations of Mozart, thankfully restored to the repertoire after two centuries of neglect.

As the typically Mozartian refrain of the last movement died away, I was curious to learn the name and number of the unfamiliar piece and particularly some information about the new recording, which I intended to purchase. As expected, the announcer's voice soon followed the music: "That was the Symphony in D by Juan Arriaga." "Who?" I exclaimed aloud. But no additional explanation was forthcoming from the radio. I at once began rummaging through all my music histories for information about this Mozart imitator. Still, he must have been a masterful imitator—he sure fooled me. Going beyond my bookshelves to the reference sections of the public library, I still discovered precious little about this Arriaga character. My curiosity was fed by the frustratingly little data I could find regarding an obviously great creator whose music, while apparently original, was indistinguishable from

Mozart's late symphonic output. Local record dealers were of no immediate help. Recordings of Arriaga's music were not readily available in most stores and had to be specially ordered. But I expected that their jacket notes would have at least some useful information about the mystery composer.

Impatient to know more, I visited the University of Minnesota's music library. Nowhere in its racks, otherwise rich in musical literature, was there a complete biography of Juan Arriaga. Apparently, the most thorough description of his life was published 164 years ago as his obituary by the long-defunct *French Revue Musicale*. But in the library's hefty tomes I found bits and pieces of information that seemed to almost arrange themselves into the story of a truly meteoritic life. They told that Juan Arriaga was remembered after his death as the Spanish Mozart. Having heard his symphony, I did not doubt it. He was actually a Basque born in Bilbao in 1806. From the incredibly early age of three, he showed outstanding musical talent, even compared to older prodigies. As an excerpt from the *French Revue Musicale* read, "he learnt [sic] the first principles of his art almost without a teacher, guided by his genius" (Hindley, p. 105). All of Bilbao turned out for the premiere of his opera. The fourteen-year-old composer was so horrified by the enormous crowd he "hid in the wings during the performance, flushed and in a state of intense panic, until a thunderous round of applause broke out in the house. He then came out of his hiding place and, extremely moved, thanked the audience with expressive bows" (Rodriguez, p. 43).

At fifteen, Arriaga journeyed to France, where he was admitted to the Paris Conservatoire as the youngest person by far ever allowed to enter the halls of that august and formidable institution. Less than three years later, he was elevated to assistant professor, likewise unprecedented for one so young. The *Encyclopedia Britannica* tells us he was a "composer of extraordinary precocity," whose music "shows abundant invention, freshness and technical resourcefulness"(H.C.R.L., p. 541). The fiery Spanish composer burst upon Paris like a comet. Almost at once, Arriaga became a musical superstar, the talk of the town. His violin performances were described as "demonic" because of the hysterical reception they invariably elicited from a rapidly growing public following. He had no interests outside his art, which obsessed as well as possessed him.

He did indeed seem perpetually entranced by music, mostly his own, and could infect others with the whirlwind charm of his highly theatrical playing. His composing abilities were no less frenetic. In the space of weeks, days, or even hours, his flaming pen spit out overtures, operas, cantatas, masses, songs, quartets, a full-length symphony, duets, chamber works, and more. As his modern biographer, José Rodriguez, wrote, "The young composer went on writing with great speed. He worked without ceasing" (p. 41). Francois J. Fetis, Arriaga's Paris teacher and postmortem champion, was no less astonished: "His progress was prodigious. The young man's progress in the art of playing the violin was no less rapid. He was endowed by nature for doing everything well in the realm of music" (Figuerido, p. 89). Arriaga's great-nephew, José, wrote of the composer, "His work was excessive and exhausting, and perhaps for that reason he caught a chest infection which, worsened by the long hours he devoted daily to his art, came to threaten his very existence" (Figuerido, p. 114). Arriaga died in 1826 just ten days short of his twentieth birthday.

To have achieved so much in such a brief lifetime seems incredible. Yet, his short-lived domination of the Parisian music scene lapsed into total eclipse with his death. In his native city, a theater was named after him and his fellow countrymen erected a monument to his memory. But the outside world knew nothing of him until recently, when new compact disc recordings are just beginning to acquaint modern listeners with his long-neglected compositions.

Compiling the scattered fragments about Arriaga somehow unsettled me. There seemed something indefinably peculiar about this personality that suddenly blazed across Western culture with such brightness and vanished just as abruptly, only to reemerge after a century and a half of obscurity via a technological medium even his stellar genius could have never envisioned. "The Spanish Mozart," I mused. His posthumous designation invited comparison.

In huge contrast to Arriaga, Wolfgang Amadeus Mozart is the most written-about musician in the world. His life and work are documented in innumerable books. In the words of the

Encyclopedia Britannica, "The Mozart literature is so vast that a mere listing of the titles would require several hundred pages" (H.C.R.L., p. 541). There are plays, movies, and even other operas about the more famous composer. At least half of the comparison would not be difficult to investigate.

Indeed, a parallel life beyond musical similarities was immediately apparent. Like Mozart, Arriaga was a child prodigy, and both were virtuoso performers who were popular sensations, however briefly. Remarkably, they shared the same first and middle names, Latin and Spanish versions, respectively, of John and Christopher. Mozart's legal name was Johannes Chrysostomus; Arriaga's was Juan Crisostomo. I wondered if the Spaniard's parents had deliberately intended him to follow in the Austrian's musical footsteps from birth. But I learned that, on the contrary, they gave him no particular direction in his life; everything that is known about Arriaga emphasizes his self-will. Neither of his parents were aware that their son's first and middle names matched Mozart's. Although his father "was very fond of music" and encouraged his boy's talent, no one in the family, except for little Juanito, showed any musical gifts or even inclinations (Figuerido, p. 5). Nor is there any evidence to indicate that he in any way consciously patterned himself after the master from Salzburg. If anything, Arriaga was his own man. Indeed, from his earliest childhood years of composition, he knew little of Mozart or any other composer. The evidence suggests Arriaga had already developed his own style before he became acquainted with Mozart's music.

Both Arriaga and Mozart were already competent musicians by their third year and mastered the violin over the clavier as their instrument of choice, itself an atypical preference for the times. Mozart composed his first opera, *Bastien und Bastienne* (K. 50), a comedy, when he was thirteen years old. *Los esclavos felices* (*The Happy Slaves*), likewise a comedy, was Arriaga's first and only opera, which he also composed "at the age of thirteen, without having formerly studied the basic principles of harmony," a virtual impossibility, according to Rodriguez (p. 38). Both left their native countries to score great popular success in Paris as composers and performers. Mozart's Paris Symphony (K. 297) was a product of his visit to the City of Lights. It was written in the key he most favored in his later symphonies, D major, the same one Arriaga preferred and used in his own Paris Symphony.

Underscoring these curious parallels is the music itself, which speaks more eloquently, although no less mysteriously, than mere coincidence. There have been many imitators of Mozart's style, conscious and unconscious. Their works were invariably distinguishable from the original, even those by very great masters. Haydn, Brahms, and even Chopin reworked Mozartian themes, but their compositions were always identifiably their own. Only Arriaga's work sounds like an organic growth directly from Mozart's compositional milieu. The connection between the music of the two composers sometimes appears seamless, even to trained ears.

Most intriguing of all, both men shared the same birthday. Mozart was born on January 27, 1756, Arriaga on January 27, 1806. While Mozart's synchronous relationship with his Spanish alter ego is described here for the first time, the case of the parallel lives of America's two most famous presidents has mystified historians for forty years. Some of the facts are obvious and well known: Both Abraham Lincoln and John Kennedy were elected the nation's chief executive exactly one hundred years apart and climaxed their respective presidencies in assassination; the vice-presidents who took over the reins of government following their murders had the same last name—Johnson. Moreover, Andrew Johnson was born in 1808, Lyndon Johnson in 1908. "Lincoln" and "Kennedy" each have seven letters (seven, as mentioned previously, signifies the completion of cycles), and both men campaigned through the unusual method of celebrated public debates with their primary opponents.

Their presidential elections were won through the narrowest of margins, and Illinois was the deciding state for both, while the question of states' rights versus civil rights was the foremost issue in their respective administrations. The name of Lincoln's personal secretary was Kennedy, while J.F.K.'s secretary was Lincoln. Continuing this twisted exchange, Lincoln's assassin shot the president in a theater and then hid in a warehouse; Oswald shot Kennedy from a warehouse and hid in a theater. And both presidents were killed on a Friday and in the presence of their wives.

Lincoln had a mystical turn of mind and took meaningful coincidences very seriously. As his biographer writes, "Throughout his life he also believed in dreams and other enigmatic signs and portents" (H.C.R.L, vol. 10, p. 986). Shortly before Lincoln's death, he told his wife about a vivid dream, in which he saw his own body laid out in a coffin draped with black crepe. Soon after his own election, Kennedy similarly anticipated his assassination with premonitory feelings (Vidal, p. 227).

The nineteenth century seems to have had its share of parallel coincidences. In 1886, the famous Apache chief Geronimo was pursued by U.S. Army Captain Henry W. Lawton. During the five months and some 1,645 miles it took him to corner his prey, Lawton became obsessed with the chase; he managed to capture Geronimo only by using deceit. Although Geronimo lived for another fourteen years, his power was broken and he died betrayed and humiliated. He never again saw his beloved Arizona homeland, which had been the real cause of his actions, primarily because of the tenacity of the U.S. soldier. Geronimo's passion for the land was due in part to the fact that it was his birthplace and in part to the generations of Apaches who had lived and died in what has since become the state of Arizona.

Meanwhile, Lawton was honored with substantial reward money and a cushy promotion as the ranking American military officer in the Philippines, where he transferred before the turn of the century. He was stationed in Manila at a palatial home with his family when a minor uprising broke out at Luzon. Although his presence was not necessary for such a minor operation, he strapped on the same Colt revolver he'd used years before in his fanatical hunt for Geronimo and led his troops into the jungle. There he was shot and killed by a sniper, who was almost immediately thereafter captured by the Americans. Upon his interrogation, the Americans were surprised to learn that the Filipino rebel's name was Geronimo.

Parallel synchronicity is not limited to famous people. Paul Kammerer, an important precursor in the scientific study of synchronicity, told of two otherwise ordinary men living parallel lives. Totally unknown and unrelated to each other, both were nevertheless born in Silesia and were volunteers in the army transport corps. In 1915, they were admitted to the same military hospital, where both were treated for pneumonia. Remarkably, they shared the same first and last names: Franz Richter.

Although, by its very nature, synchronicity is a very personal phenomenon, I have tried, with as few exceptions as possible, to distance myself from the investigation. It is with some reluctance then, that I cite the following case as an example. Like the Mozart-Arriaga comparison, it has never been published before, and were it not such an effective representative of the category here described, I would not include it.

In early 1988, I happened to come across a brief biographical sketch of Ignatius Donnelly, an American writer and politician who lived during the second half of the nineteenth century. It seems strange that I neglected to learn anything about him considering he is the founder of Atlantology, the modern study of the Atlantis legend, which had by that time absorbed much of my thought. I had read his book, *Atlantis: The Antediluvian World*, many times, but I never bothered about the man himself. My own book on the subject was already a year old. But casually looking over the account of Donnelly's life for the first time, I was mildly surprised to learn that we shared the same birthday—November 3. Ignorant of synchronicity at the time, I regarded the parallel as a happy coincidence, nothing more. Assuming it would amuse my mother, I pointed out his biography. But the expression that came over her face was not one of amusement. Following a pause to get over her astonishment, she told me something about my birth I had never known before. And what she told me changed my life forever.

She said that before I was born, a serious effort was made on her side of the family to name me after the patron saint of the local school—Ignatius. Father Vaughn, my grandmother's very close friend, urged that I be so baptized. But my mother resisted the pressure of friends and relatives and I was christened after a saint with a less archaic name. To have been born on the same day as the foremost writer on Atlantis might have been a pleasant happenstance. But (almost) sharing the same first name suggested something else, something far beyond my ability to even begin to understand. The comparison chilled me with wonder. I wanted to learn if there were any more significant parallels between Ignatius Donnelly and myself.

I went to Saint Paul, where the Minnesota Historical Society preserved all of his published books and private papers, including his diaries, which were supplemented by a number of modern biographies. I got to know him quite well in the ensuing months and years. Sometimes I felt so overwhelmed I grew faint with the number and kind of coincidental comparisons between this man and myself. Not only was it easy to find things in his life that had already been paralleled in mine, but coincidences linking him and me were still taking place.

For example, his horrific vision of the twentieth century was contained in a novel, *Caesar's Column*, written in the mid-1880s and last republished in the 1960s. The public interlibrary loan system took several months to locate a copy, which finally arrived in September 1988. When I opened it, the first page explained that the events depicted in the book are supposed to take place in the month of September 1988.

That same year, some friends gave me a gold pen with my name inscribed on one side. Months afterward, I read in a Donnelly biography that he had been presented with an inscribed gold pen exactly one hundred years earlier. In May 1988, I traveled to Ireland for the first time. When I returned some months later, another biography was waiting for me. In it, I read that Donnelly had sailed to Ireland for the first time in May 1888.

In 1995, without my having applied, a small Minnesota publishing company offered me a job only a few miles from Nininger, the same place where Donnelly spent most of his life and wrote all his books, his most famous being *Atlantis: The Antediluvian World*. While in the nearby Minnesota town, I finished my own book on the same subject, *The Destruction of Atlantis*, which I'd begun eight years before I knew anything about Donnelly. Only after its completion did I learn that he had originally entitled his book *The Destruction of Atlantis*. The day before I bicycled to Nininger for the first time, my employer, who knew nothing about my planned outing, gave me a magazine about Minnesota. She had never done anything of the kind before. "I don't know why," she said, "but I felt compelled to buy this for you." Although she was absolutely ignorant of its contents and there was nothing on its cover to indicate the subjects contained inside, the magazine featured an article about Ignatius Donnelly and Nininger. The man and the town are today only very rarely featured in any periodicals, even in their own state.

The only clue, or so it seemed, to this ongoing mystery appeared to be Donnelly's death. He died just as the bells all over Saint Paul were ringing in the new year of 1901. To paraphrase one of his biographers, he passed away precisely at the moment the century he wrote about came into being (McHenry, p. 275). Something inexpressible seemed suggested by the timing of his death. Reading that a heart condition had literally choked him into the next world, I thought of what I had been told about my own birth. Apparently, while still inside the womb, I had somehow gotten the umbilical cord wrapped several times around my neck. Every time the effort was made at birthing, it tightened around my throat, choking me. At one point I was half in and half out and still being strangled by the tenacious umbilical. Only with some difficulty and much skill was the doctor able to cut it and free me. Donnelly choked in death. I choked in birth. Did all this mean he was a previous incarnation?

When I found his grave in a suburban cemetery and stood by the headstone, I felt nothing special. Back at the Minnesota Historical Society, I touched the desk at which Donnelly wrote and handled certain of his personal effects, including a leather traveling bag. There was no rush of past-life memories, no sense of familiarity. Cases of reincarnation I'd studied bore little or no resemblance to the coincidences I was observing in my own life. Moreover, people who claimed past-life memories never reported the kind of synchronicities I'd experienced connecting two individuals separated by a hundred years. No, reincarnation and parallel lives were two different animals. Parallel lives are those in which two (occasionally more) people otherwise completely separated by blood relation or time share extraordinary meaningful commonalities. Reincarnation is the recurrence of one lifetime after another experienced by the same human soul. Reincarnated people report strong feelings of familiarity with the past, even recognition of bygone details from another time. None of that was part of my Donnelly experience.

After nearly ten years of personal investigation, I have still to find credible explanations of this enigma. But the search for answers has not been without reward, because it led me to question the entire subject of synchronicity. Parallel lives represent an actual phenomenon that can be verified by hard data. They also simultaneously provide a sense of destiny and awe for those aware of the connecting details. Beyond these determinations, they may lead one into a philosophical and spiritual quest for the truth. For example, growing awareness of my own acausal connection with Ignatius Donnelly prepared me for the event that sparked a lifelong study of synchronicity—namely, my encounter with the car bearing the Rushdie license plate.

But parallel lives do not only connect the present with the past, the living with the dead. They also occur between contemporary individuals. A 1978 story that appeared in the *San Francisco Chronicle* told of two unrelated Maryland women with an identical name, Wanda Marie Johnson. Until introduced by a reporter, they had never met. Born on the same day, June 15, 1953, both were the eldest of two sisters and one brother. Both Wandas were former residents of the District of Columbia before moving to Prince Georges County, where they were the mothers of two children. Both attended the Howard Clinic, whose Howard University Hospital was the scene for the births of their babies. Both owned 1977 two-door Ford Grenadas, the eleven-digit serial numbers of which were the same minus the last three. Their social security numbers had the same first four digits, and the following two, although transposed, were the same ("Two Lives, a Weird Coincidence," p. 12).

One of the most illustrious cases of parallel lives involved Italy's king at the turn of the century. On July 28, 1900, Umberto I was introduced to a man who not only shared his name but was born on the same day in Turin, the monarch's birthplace. The stranger even bore a striking physical resemblance to Umberto, and both men were married to women with the same name, Margherita. The following day, the king learned that his double had been shot to death in an accident. A few hours later, Umberto himself was assassinated by an anarchist's bullet (Hicks, p. 125).

A historian in my research group, Dr. Alfred Walker, from the University of Wisconsin at Greenbay, was writing about an American bomber pilot who crashed in Germany during World War I. The pilot managed to elude capture for nine days before being apprehended and confined to an internment camp for the duration of the war. While in the process of describing the airman's plight, Walker received a telephone call from a friend who knew nothing of his work in progress. He called to tell the historian about a colleague whose story he thought would make an interesting book. It was the autobiography of a World War II U.S. bomber pilot who crashed in Germany, where he escaped capture for nine days before being confined until the end of hostilities as a prisoner of war. This case of double synchronicity contains elements of parallel lives and parallel work. Both men were concerned with strikingly similar books at the same moment.

Many of the persons involved in these instances of parallel lives shared common birthdays, a leading element in this peculiar form occasionally taken by synchronicity. An outstanding example was reported by Evelyn Diebold, from Muldelein, Illinois. She was born on May 24, 1940. That her daughter, Victoria, was born on May 24, 1961 is curious enough, until we learn that in addition to this meaningful coincidence, Evelyn's great uncle, (1891), nephew Dale (1957), niece Kathy (1967), and second cousins Bud (1946), Tom (1970), and Arthur (1991) were all born on May 24!

Among the most famous examples of parallel work took place in the mid-nineteenth century, with the simultaneous development of the theory of the origin of species. While Charles Darwin was secretly writing *Origin of the Species* in London, he was shocked to receive a manuscript that virtually mirrored his own conclusions on evolution and natural selection. It was written on the other side of the world, in the Malay Archipelago, by Alfred Russell Wallace, who was working independently from Darwin, without a clue about the older man's research. Remarking that even some of Wallace's leading terms were already included as chapter headings in his book, Darwin said, "I never saw a more striking coincidence." As their contemporary, Ralph Waldo Emerson, noticed, "Certain ideas are in the air. We are all impressionable, for we are made of them; all impressionable, but some more than others, and these first express them. This explains the curious contemporaneousness of inventions and discoveries" (Emerson, p. 666).

Less well known is the parallel invention of the first self-contained underwater breathing apparatus (scuba), or Aqua-Lung, in the United States by the Milwaukee deep-sea diver Max Knohl and Jacques Cousteau, in France. Neither knew of the other's existence, much less their work on the same project.

In the 1970s, a would-be playwright in my research group accidentally found a rare old book that described the biography of David Merrick, a man who was horribly disfigured from birth but possessed a fine mind and kind heart. Merrick passed from sideshow freak into genuine renown and respect until his early death. My friend had never encountered the story before and, seeing its dramatic potential, began turning it into what he assumed would be a most unique theatrical drama. While in the process of organizing his material, he was surprised and disappointed to read about the debut of a new play about David Merrick. It was called *The Elephant Man*.

In our earlier discussion of animal ostenta, I introduced Mike Solarzano whose coincidental photograph of a whale spurred his interest in Pacific archaeology. Apparently, his synchronicity led to another meaningful coincidence after his return home from Oahu. As he reported in his own words, "In May 1996, I began feeling a sudden, even powerful, interest in all things Lemurian. My thoughts kept gravitating of their own accord in that direction, and I found myself constantly seeking out information on the subject. One evening, while thinking I should telephone a friend likewise interested in the sunken Pacific Ocean civilization, he called, something of a synchronicity itself. When I mentioned to him that I had felt strongly drawn to things Lemurian recently, he told me he'd felt the same compulsion over the last several days, too. After comparing notes, we learned that our simultaneous fascination with Lemuria coincided the previous May 9 with a Roman festival known as the Lemuria. Neither of us had known before the date on which the festival took place. We felt that our common upsurge of interest in the subject was somehow connected through an ancient festival of the same name."

Certain ideas that acausally and simultaneously materialize in the minds of human beings are said to be "in the air." Is this a popular admission that telepathy is the real connecting principle between otherwise unrelated people? Or is even this paranormal agency inadequate to fully account for the larger phenomenon of synchronicity?

Parallelism can link not only individuals in a common fate but whole nations, an observation that was made by the early-twentieth-century philosopher Oswald Spengler. He noticed that every previous civilization—ancient and modern, Western and Eastern—appeared to undergo the same general pattern of birth, youth, maturity, middle age, decline, and extinction. Society is the macrocosm of the individual, subjected to the same cycles as a mortal human. The belief that history repeats itself seemed borne out by the numerous examples Spengler cited in *The Decline of the West*. Sometimes, the recurring patterns are remarkably similar.

In the past, a people whose emblem was the swastika arose as the dominant power on the continent. Their enemies in the west became allies and crossed the sea in a huge invasion fleet to land on the shores of the occupied territories. After a long, bitter war, the soldiers of the swastika were killed or taken prisoner and their capital destroyed by fire. While these lines bring to mind the Normandy Invasion of Hitler's Europe in 1944 and its climax one year later in Berlin, they fit just as accurately a war that took place 3,200 years before, when the Trojans, whose surviving cultural artifacts are typically emblazoned with the swastika, dominated most of Asia Minor. They were overcome in a long struggle with the allied peoples of the Greek Peninsula, who sailed across the Aegean Sea in "a thousand ships" to invade Troy and eventually incinerate its chief city, Ilios. Whether Hitler knew that the swastika was emblematic of Troy is incidental to his reason for choosing it as his movement's symbol, which he associated with the Indo-European ancestors of the German people.

The politically exploitative side of synchronicity has been recognized in the past and is acknowledged even today by government leaders. They use historical parallels as propaganda to justify their ideological causes. When, for example, the Germans and Japanese went to war against the United States in 1941, Nazi mystics argued that their common struggle was providentially symbolized in the national flags flown by the respective combatants. The swastika, they pointed out, was previously an ancient symbol for solar deities, such as the Greek god Apollo, whose temple at Antinopolis, in the Lower Nile Valley, was decorated with the hooked cross. The other solar symbol was Imperial Japan's flag of the rising sun. By contrast, the national colors of the United States featured a field of stars in the night sky. The "predestined" symbolism of these three national flags was interpreted by Third Reich propagandists to mean that the Axis forces of light and enlightenment were fighting the powers of darkness. Germany and Japan were, consequently, depicted as sharing a parallel destiny through the synchronicity of their prehistoric, national emblems.

At the time, the Allies perceived an entirely different synchronicity in the same flags. The swastika was portrayed in numerous wartime posters as a broken crucifix, signifying the deliberate destruction of Christian civilization. Japan's flag was characterized not as the sun but as a grasping octopus rising from the sea, a subconscious expression of Japanese imperialism. The stars of the American flag, on the other hand, were regarded as universal archetypes of hope for the peoples of the world who were conquered by or still fought the Axis.

I give these mid-twentieth-century comparisons to show how the authority of meaningful coincidences affected the psychology of whole nations striving to empower their sense of self. Often, they perceived the apparent parallel lives of certain peoples sharing a common destiny. Flags are potent images expressing the identity and distilling the character of the particular peoples they signify into a single, powerful image. As such, they are open to the passions, and sometimes the hysteria, of the group consciousness, which may use interpretations of national synchronicity to justify political ambitions.

Perhaps the historical periodicity Spengler detected in the broad cycles of civilization is the same cycle operating on a microcosmic level among individual human beings. If so, then the organizational principle of the universe makes no distinction between energy and matter but orders the seen, as well as the unseen, into some cosmic scheme that we know exists but is too colossal for us to comprehend. We are a single, painted stone in a mosaic as broad as all existence. We may sometimes find other colored stones together with which we comprise a complete image. But the whole mosaic is far too enormous for us to envision in its entirety. We lack the objectivity of its creator to see the mural in its perfect perspective, which is the only viewpoint from which we could learn the whole truth.

The undeniable fact that parallel lives occur demonstrates that certain individuals share a common destiny through their mutual identities, even though they may be physically separated by distance and death. We may conclude from parallel lives that they represent dramatic evidence on behalf of synchronicity as a principle, a power; they are evidence of the cosmic mind or will that transcends space and time to connect us with a mystery beyond understanding. Acknowledging the existence of parallel lives informs us, at least, that we are not annihilated by the inevitable loss of our physical existence. Instead, we share personally in the eternity of time itself.

chapter 5

Life Imitates Art

*At the conjuror's, we detect the hair by which he moves
his puppet, but we have not eyes sharp enough to descry
the thread that ties cause and effect.*

—Ralph Waldo Emerson, *Fate*

The Indian Vedas quoted in chapter 1 tell us that while music, painting, poetry, sculpture, and architecture comprise the art created by humans, nature is God's art. Consequently, the Vedas argue, the closer our art approaches nature, the closer it and we, who experience it, come to God. For the Hindu ancient writers, then, the highest expressions of art transcended mere entertainment or edification to reach for something higher and spiritually grander. Supreme creations like the Taj Mahal or the *Mahābhārata* were regarded by them as humankind's noblest attempts at meeting the Creator halfway. This extra-aesthetic ability of art to rise above and beyond itself was restated by Shakespeare, who has Hamlet say that the best art should "hold the mirror up to nature." To be sure, the most influential instances of art induce precisely those altered states of human consciousness wherein synchronicity manifests itself. Through the power of catharsis, art brings us into the world of myth, using a skillfully organized collage of archetypes, a parade of symbolic images tripping thousands of psychological switches to conjure the deepest emotions.

It should come as no surprise, then, that people who create art, as well as those who simply enjoy it, often find themselves used as involuntary vehicles for meaningful coincidence. The making of art is an exercise of the imaginative faculty, which itself operates from subconscious origins. Surrealist art unabashedly attempts to mirror the dream state, while Richard Wagner's *Ring Cycle* of music-dramas is positively clairvoyant: Its *Twilight of the Gods* was acted out on the world stage of 1945, seventy years after it was first performed on the smaller German stage at Bayreuth.

That extramusical drama began to take shape in the years preceding World War I. At that time, Adolf Hitler was a poverty-stricken day laborer with dreams of becoming an artist. Sharing his obscurity with an equally destitute music student, August Kubiczek, his only friend and confidant, he could barely afford an occasional, standing-room-only ticket for the theater. One night he and Kubiczek went to the Austrian city of Linz, where a rare performance of Wagner's early, less frequently staged work was being presented. Seeing and hearing *Rienzi, the Last of the Tribunes* would be a new experience for the two impoverished opera-goers. It turned out to be far more than a novelty for both of them.

Rienzi is the story of a fourteenth-century statesman who raises his fellow Romans from their degenerated society through the power of his oratory. Uniting all classes in a patriotic revolution against the corrupt aristocrats, he overthrows their wicked regime and builds another state on the glory of ancient Rome. For a time, his new order is a popular success and Italy rises to its former greatness. A war against the émigré aristocrats ensues, Rienzi is victorious, and the masses hail him as their Tribune. But the surviving nobles agitate a subversive propaganda campaign among the people, the Church turns against Rienzi, and he is the near-victim of an unsuccessful assassination. His popular favor erodes, and even his closest comrades desert him. In the end, he is left alone in the capitol surrounded by a huge, torch-bearing mob. Mussolinilike, he harangues his benighted opponents from the balcony, prophesying that as long as the seven hills of Rome stand, he will return in some distant future to renew their greatness. With that, the incensed crowd hurls brands into the capitol building, which erupts with a conflagration. Rienzi vanishes among the fire, as Wagner's music graphically depicts flames soaring into the night sky.

That so twentieth-century a work was composed as long ago as 1840 is itself a remarkably clairvoyant act. Its effect on the twenty-year-old Hitler, however, was traumatic. He had been inspired by art before, especially Wagner's art. But this was something altogether different. After the performance he looked visibly shaken. Kubiczek asked what was the matter with him. "Shut up and follow me!" was his answer. They walked for more than half an hour in silence, eventually reaching the top of the Freinberg, a high hill in the public park overlooking Linz.

When they reached the top, Hitler seized his friend's hands and spoke as he never had before. As he gazed off into the night sky, his torrent of words seemed to belong to a man possessed. Kubiczek felt he was not even speaking to him, that he spoke as though he were addressing some huge crowd that was visible only to himself. Still vibrating with the effect produced in him by the *Rienzi* performance, a transfigured Hitler spoke as though in a trance, saying that one day he would be "given a mandate by the whole German people" to unite them as never before and lead them to unprecedented heights of ideological, military, social, and cultural greatness. The struggle would be extremely perilous, with dangers all around, just as dramatized in the opera. Everything could collapse in terrible destruction, but his high destiny would nevertheless be fulfilled. Kubiczek might have laughed out loud had his friend not been in such deadly earnest.

Here was an utterly obscure, impoverished, undernourished, failed artist, peddling water colors for a few coins, with no other friends, no helpful relatives. Yet, standing in his threadbare clothes, he was convinced a future of earthshaking magnitude lay ahead for him. He and Kubiczek never spoke of his strange behavior again.

Just before World War I began, they parted company, and they did not meet until the advent of another war, in 1939. Kubiczek, now a disabled veteran, was able to speak alone with his old friend, who had since become the führer of the Third Reich. For the first time in twenty-seven years, Kubiczek reminded him of that night in Linz and the *Rienzi* performance. In response, Hitler looked thoughtfully out the window of the private room in which they were waiting for his motorcade. After a long moment of heavy silence, he said in a quiet voice, "In that moment it began" (Kubiczek, p. 193).

Many of his biographers have commented on Hitler's apparent sixth sense, particularly when deadly danger threatened him. The odds against his survival as a frontline soldier and courier from the very beginning of World War I to its conclusion, four years later, were astronomical. Of all those who made up his List Regiment in 1914, he and only one other man survived. There were many eye-witness accounts by both officers and enlisted men of his precognitive ability to know, often within seconds, precisely where a shell would go off. On November 9, 1939, speaking at a meeting in Munich, Hitler unaccountably cut short his traditionally long speech to Party veterans of the 1923 Putsch and quickly left the hall. Minutes later, a powerful bomb, secreted inside a wood pillar before which he had just concluded his remarks, detonated, killing several people.

Five years later, another bomb exploded in a conference room where he was planning strategy with his commanders. Men standing next to him died or were severely wounded. Hitler only lost his trousers and most of the hearing in one ear. Seconds before the bomb went off, he had been standing directly over it. At the last moment, the briefcase containing the deadly device was inadvertently moved aside by someone else.

Although born and raised in the Catholic Church, to which he appears to have been devoted until the early 1930s, Hitler eventually drifted away from institutionalized religion. After he became chancellor in 1933, his public speeches and particularly his private conversations referred less to Jesus and Christianity than to a beneficent, although indefinite, Providence that had always guided and shielded him. To the end, he maintained a strong sense of his own destiny.

There are psychological and esoteric, even occult, interpretations of Hitler's apparently paranormal experiences. Marie-Louise von Franz, Jung's colleague, who became well known after Jung's death through her public lectures, believed that the Germans, in their miserable situation following World War I, began "to constellate in the unconscious...the savior-hero archetype," a mass "projection" that fell onto "a criminal psychopath" (von Franz, p. 56). Hitler was thus empowered, if not actually created, by the wish fulfillment of an entire people, in which the national fate of one was indistinguishable from the personal Providence of the other.

Even "hysterical psychopaths" of less infamy are credited with similarly providential coincidences. For example, the noted psychiatrist Arnold Mindel knew a patient who announced himself as Jesus Christ and claimed he could create or destroy light. The megalomaniac had just made this declaration when he was struck unconscious by a light fixture falling from the ceiling (Peat, pp. 27, 28).

Some modern writers conclude that Hitler somehow tapped into the dark side of his own subconscious to release latent paranormal powers in a pact with the Devil to rule the world. He was thus a Satanist. Hitler stole from a Vienna museum an object called the Spear of Destiny (the lance that was supposed to have pierced the side of Christ on the cross), with which he was able to alter the warp and woof of destiny, thus suiting his own diabolical purposes (Cranston, p. 28).

Initiates of esoteric traditions, both Eastern and Western, claim that each human being is born with all the knowledge of the entire universe, but only in moments of rare lucidity does some of that higher information break through to our consciousness. They would conclude that Hitler, in reacting so passionately to *Rienzi*, correctly envisioned his future, which had been likewise envisioned and dramatized in the opera. When he saw the Linz performance, his soul simply recognized its destiny acted out on the stage years in advance.

Whether or not one chooses to accept this interpretation, such far-ranging coincidences—from the precognitive *Rienzi* to Hitler's prophetic reaction and his subsequent life—suggest that impassioned people enter deep, altered states of consciousness, from which they do indeed access the paranormal. Having fallen into this altered frame of mind, Hitler subconsciously decoded Wagner's own artistic trance state, preserved in the details of his opera. It was as though two men, one long dead, were communicating together through their dreams. In any case, *Rienzi, the Last of the Roman Tribunes* gives us an especially potent example of synchronicity operating through music and drama, a world-changing instance of life imitating art.

Despite the electrifying drama of synchronous events carried along by music, nothing surpasses in natural magic the mysterious coincidences afforded by literature. And no other author is more appropriately linked to the phenomenon than Edgar Allan Poe—which comes as no surprise, in view of his famous paranormal tales and poetry. In *The Mystery of Marie Roget*, he wrote,

> *There are few persons, even among the calmest thinkers, who have not occasionally been startled into a vague yet thrilling half-credence in the supernatural by coincidences of so seemingly marvelous a character that, as mere coincidences, the intellect has been unable to receive them.*
>
> *Such sentiments—for the half-credences of which I speak have never the full force of thought—such sentiments are seldom thoroughly stifled unless by reference to the doctrine of chance, or, as it is technically termed, the Calculus of Probabilities. Now this Calculus is, in its essence, purely mathematical; and thus we have the anomaly of the most rigidly exact in science applied to the shadow and spirituality of the most intangible in speculation.* (Poe, p. 174)

What makes Poe's thoughtful interest in meaningful coincidence all the more intriguing is his role in an extraordinary case of synchronicity he never lived to know about. His novelette, *The Narrative of Arthur Gordon Pym of Nantucket*, is the story of three men cast adrift in an open boat after their vessel is sunk in a storm. Starving to death and driven mad by hunger, they kill the cabin boy, Richard Parker, and eat him. Poe's long prose work was published as original fiction in 1838. Forty-six years later, and thirty-five years after Poe's death, three shipwrecked survivors in an open boat cannibalized a fourth, the cabin boy, whose name was none other than Richard Parker. At their trial in 1884, Poe's story was cited in connection with the accused, but the uneducated seamen were not familiar with it. Neither the prosecution nor the defense could determine any relationship that the story might have to the trial, other than a most wildly circumstantial one, and further mention of it in the court testimonies was dropped (Poe, p. 286).

Like Wagner, and in an altogether different art form, Poe envisioned a future event without consciously recognizing his own precognition. How could he, having died before it came to pass? His mind had been caught in the grip of the creative process that, especially for masters of great ability, went so deep into his subconscious that he was able to bring back from the future something seen with the inner eye of his soul. His prophetic story again demonstrates that deeply altered states of consciousness tap into the universal mechanism of the cosmos to bring about synchronous events.

The implication of such involuntary shamanistic adventures is that linear concepts of time are entirely subjective, seen from our limited perspective in a material dimension. In the far broader objectivity available to Otherworldly travelers like Wagner and Poe, time appears all of one piece in what Kant referred to as "an Eternal Present." As it is described in the ancient traditions of the Hindus and Norse, time is like an ever-turning wheel, on which all things come, go, and return, perpetually. An old and commonly heard saying, "Great events cast their own shadows ahead of themselves," demonstrates to what degree the notion of precognition occupies popular thinking.

But Poe was not alone in writing a fictional account of a disaster at sea that actually came to pass years later. In 1898, British author Morgan Robertson published the novel *The Wreck of the Titan; or, Futility*. It is the story of an oceanliner on her maiden voyage from England. She is the largest, fastest, most luxurious of her kind ever built, and her captain is out to set a speed record to New York. Departing in April, he guides the *Titan* through the northernmost shipping lanes of the Atlantic, where her lookouts spot an iceberg. Too late, she strikes it amidships, tearing several gashes in her hull below the water line near the watertight doors, the most vulnerable section of the ship. Panic ensues aboard when passengers and crew realize there are not enough lifeboats for everyone. The vessel deemed "unsinkable" by its makers goes down, exacting a horrible death toll.

All this sounds eerily familiar to us at a time when our society appears obsessed with the lost *Titanic*. Its deep-water discovery in 1986 continues to generate scientific debate over the disaster, and there are countless new books reexamining its every aspect, as well as museum recreations, feature films, even a musical. What is it we see in this doomed vessel that somehow mirrors ourselves? And what did Morgan Robertson envision a full fourteen years before the event? Comparison of his novel and the real-life event it foreshadowed outstrips all rational estimates for coincidental probability.

The nineteenth-century author described his fictional ship as eight hundred feet long, with three propellers (a highly unusual configuration, then and later) that drove her at twenty-four knots against the iceberg; the *Titanic* was 882.5 feet long, also had three propellers, and struck the iceberg at twenty-two knots. She carried only twenty lifeboats, four fewer than her literary predecessor. Both ships were wrecked in the month of April. Finally, and most powerfully, there is the chilling similarity of the ships' names.

Nor was Robertson the only author to prefigure the sinking of the *Titanic*. Five years before his book was published, the still-to-be-famous German writer Gerhard Hauptmann wrote *Atlantis*, a novel about a super oceanliner, the *Roland*. Hauptmann describes the ship as "unsinkable" and repeatedly uses the adjective "titanic" to point up its unprecedented size. During a transatlantic crossing bound for New York, the *Roland* sinks, with terrible loss of life, after a mysterious collision that is never fully explained.

Atlantis originally had very limited circulation in Germany, so it is highly unlikely that Robertson, who, in any case, could not read German and never mentioned Hauptmann's novel, was influenced by his contemporary on the Continent. Moreover, *The Wreck of the Titan* contains far many more details in common with the actual sinking. But after the turn of the century, Hauptmann achieved an international reputation and most of his earlier works were republished in various languages throughout the world. Remarkably, his *Atlantis*, with its "titanic" *Roland*, was released in its first English edition at the beginning of 1912, the same year in which the disaster occurred just a few months later.

Far more typical of the premonitions that seemed to constellate around the *Titanic* were overwhelming feelings of foreboding experienced by some passengers and would-be passengers, who irrationally canceled their bookings shortly before boarding or engaged in similarly irrational behavior which somehow prefigured what was to come. Even more numerous were precognitive dreams associated with the disaster.

A particularly unusual intuition occurred during the *Titanic*'s death throes in the North Atlantic. At the same moment, unknown to anyone else in the outside world, in far-away Scotland, a young girl lay dying at Kirkendbright's Salvation Army hospital. In her delirium, she suddenly grasped the hand of an attendant standing by her bedside and implored him, "Captain, can't you see that big ship sinking? Look at all those people drowning! Someone called Willy is playing a fiddle and coming at you." These were virtually her last words before she passed away. Only a few hours later, the attendant learned of the disaster in which his brother, Willy, perished as a violinist of the doomed oceanliner's band.

During her altered state of consciousness, the dying girl had merged the otherwise apparently inviolable boundaries of space and time to personally participate in a major human event. In short, with her soul or consciousness already hovering between physical and nonphysical realities in that unknown midregion inhabited by synchronous phenomena, she was momentarily privy to both worlds.

These reality shifts appear to jolt forward into the future more often than slide into the past, perhaps because matters of life and death, which contain the most meaning and therefore psychic energy, occur in the context of present and future time. Another example is *The China Syndrome*, a fictional movie about a nuclear disaster in which an atomic power plant suffers a meltdown. Just three weeks after the film's debut, the incident became reality at Pennsylvania's infamous Three Mile Island nuclear facility.

Synchronicities of this staggering magnitude leave us with few alternative interpretations. If Robertson did not subconsciously envision a future event in his novel, perhaps he intuited the real nature of time itself, in which there is no past, present, or future. Instead, time is a state of being in which everything is frozen into happening altogether and at once, constantly and eternally. Such a view would explain why people who know about disasters before they occur are unable to prevent them from happening. It is not only that such events will happen, but that they have already taken place and are actually occurring now at another, related level of invisible existence or dimension glimpsed only now and then by people like Poe and Robertson.

If so, then the likelihood that there is such a thing as individual free will grows questionable. We might be laboring under an illusion when we presume that we are in control of our lives. All the things that happen to us and every action we undertake might seem like random occurrences or personal decisions, but instead our entire experience and behavior might be no less inextricably locked into the universal organizing principle of existence than the very cells of our own bodies. If so, then there is no escaping destiny, because it and we are interwoven together in the same fabric. All we can do is recognize it. Synchronicity is the tear in the veil, the sudden, unexpectedly revealing connection between that Otherworld always turning behind the scenes of this one, like the backstage goings-on of a play that the audience is not supposed to see.

This perspective raises disturbing questions that shake our fundamental perceptions of the world and our individual place in it. The answers we learn from meaningful coincidence might very well force us to radically revise established notions about existence itself.

Poe was not the only visionary writer of the nineteenth century. A novelist known for his prophetic novels was Jules Verne. In *Master of the World* (1886), he foresaw the use of zeppelins as warships of the air in World War I. In *Twenty Thousand Leagues Under the Sea* (1870), he envisioned scuba gear and atomic-powered submarines, while *From the Earth to the Moon* (1873) described space travel. In a conscious act of meaningful coincidence, the world's first nuclear-powered submarine was christened in 1955 the U.S.S. *Nautilus*, after Captain Nemo's vessel. In 1996, a lost, previously unpublished and unknown Verne work, written more than one hundred years before, was discovered by literary researchers at Amiens, where Verne spent his last days. *Paris in the Twentieth Century* portrayed the French people of 1988, when mass transit is entirely motorized, fax machines are in every office and many homes, and birth-control pills are commonly used by both married and unmarried women—an unthinkable abomination for Verne's Victorian contemporaries, whose sensitivities may have dissuaded him from publishing what was then sure to be regarded as a scandalous novel.

Coincidentally, Ignatius Donnelly also wrote a novel about life in 1988. *Caesar's Column* describes poison gas, radio, television, the rise of Africa's third-world powers (the story begins in the independent nation of Uganda, a lowly, obscure British colony in 1891, when the novel was first published), and worldwide mass transportation. Donnelly even coined the term "airline" to describe transatlantic air service—this a dozen years before the Wright brothers' first flight at Kitty Hawk.

In the previous century, Irish author Jonathan Swift described the moons of Mars more than 150 years before they were discovered in 1877 by the U.S. Naval Observatory. In his 1726 novel, *Gulliver's Travels*, Swift accurately portrayed the Martian satellites as very tiny; the diameters of Deimos and Phobos are just sixteen and ten kilometers, respectively.

Synchronistic art does not always connect with disaster or prophetic developments, however. More often, it comments upon daily affairs, traumatic as they may sometimes be. For example, a Chicago business executive caught in downtown traffic was sitting in his car at an intersection, when an Oldsmobile ran the red light in front of him. He watched, horrified, as the large vehicle lost control and jumped the curb, running over a little girl and throwing her mother violently against the stone wall of a skyscraper. Incredibly, the woman seemed unhurt, but her daughter was obviously dead. Her mother screamed with a voice that overrode all the mechanical cacophony of the city. The man had never heard a sound like that in his life. Her wail cut like a dagger blade deep into some sensitive part of him he did not know existed until he felt it.

Everything happened before his eyes in a matter of seconds, as though in some kind of monstrous slow motion. Now the light changed and a policeman waved him through. But he was so emotionally shaken that he pulled off to park on a side street as soon as possible. Unable to drive for another twenty minutes, he could not purge from his mind the horror of the scene he had just witnessed. Then, almost involuntarily, he felt a black anger welling up inside him, an anger against God. How, for all His reputed mercy, could He have allowed such a thing to happen? Where were His alleged guardian angels when they were most needed? At that moment, desperate to get his thoughts off the accident, he switched on the radio. The music that came on was an orchestral section from *Hansel and Gretel*. It described a scene in the opera in which the two children are asleep in the forest, as guardian angels descend and watch over them. This coincidence somehow evaporated his anger with God, while a calm, nameless assurance settled on his nerves. And he knew somehow that the little girl was all right in a way beyond reason. Self-composed, he drove the rest of the way home. Once there, he lit a single candle on behalf of the unknown mother and child. In this instance, the musical synchronicity effected a kind of transcendent healing and reconciled the observer to a traumatic event that would have otherwise almost certainly deepened his spiritual bitterness. His story was among the most touching instances of synchronicity related by anyone in our group of contributors. Most of them felt equally, if not always quite so profoundly, changed for the better through such mystical encounters, as in the following examples.

A man going to work in his car one March afternoon was listening to an audiocassette he'd picked up recently from the local library. The recording featured C. Day Lewis reading *The Christmas Tree*, his poem comparing the tree to the impermanence of life and the short-lived nature of all joy. His recitation had just begun, when the driver noticed a pathetic-looking Christmas tree discarded at the side of the road, an unusual sight so long after the holiday. Strangely perhaps, the effect of this synchronicity was not to make him despair that happiness was a transient phenomenon. Instead, it reminded him that one should make good use of one's time, find pleasure in life, and avoid wasting opportunities for enjoyment.

Paul Westerberg, a Wisconsin salesman who had driven over a thousand miles in what seemed a fruitless trip, was returning home along the same expressway that had brought him so far south. To get his mind off his disappointment, he randomly selected a tape for the cassette deck. After three or four other numbers, some music about the Spanish city of Grenada began to play. Just at that moment, he passed a sign for the next town, Grenada, Mississippi. While hardly an earthshaking coincidence, the synchronicity made him feel that somehow, in the grander scheme of his life, even this apparently wasted trip was part of an overall strategy he could not see or understand, but that nevertheless existed. Nothing, Westerberg felt, was without significance or purpose.

Sometimes, a particular synchronicity will repeat itself like a musical refrain, until the person to whom it is directed takes notice. Wayne Taylor, a businessman on his lunch break, wandered into a store to look over its selection of books. He found himself enjoying some unfamiliar atmospheric music played over the speakers. Instead of a new book, he purchased a cassette of *The Standing Stones of Callanish*, composed and performed by New Zealander Jon Mark, describing a four-thousand-year-old megalithic site among the Hebrides, off Scotland's west coast. Returning to work, Taylor was approached by a friend from Glasgow, who, unaware of his recent purchase, showed him a large photograph of the Callanish stones in the copy of a travel magazine.

Years later, just as he was reading a book about Callanish and wondering how he could get there on his limited finances, he received a telephone call from another store, informing him that *The Standing Stones of Callanish* had arrived under his name, even though he had not ordered another copy. When he finally did travel to Scotland, he visited another Neolithic ruin located on a high, lonely hill just outside of and overlooking the city of Inverness, in the north. Popularly known as the Druids' Temple, the site appealed to his sense of tranquillity, and he lingered in the ancient megalithic circle for most of the pleasant May afternoon.

Hoping to get the best angle for a good photograph of the site, Taylor propped his back up against the largest of the stones, a twelve-foot-high granite block interlined with veins of white crystal. His position afforded a perfect view of the temple. When he returned home weeks later, his Glasgow friend told him he had had a fleeting, although arresting vision of him leaning up against a stone wall while he was overseas. Consulting the journal he kept of his travels, he learned that his friend's vision coincided with the date and hour he had his back to the great monolith of the Druids' Temple.

As mentioned earlier, the creative and recreative processes for both those who make art and others who experience it induce altered states of consciousness in which these people seem to subconsciously tap into the oversoul of the universe. Such aesthetic overlap often results in meaningful coincidences that connect our mundane lives with the Otherworld.

At the 1791 London premier of a new symphony by Franz Joseph Haydn, members of the audience were so taken with the music that, after the first movement, they picked up their chairs and gathered closer around the orchestra, leaving an empty space near the middle of the hall. Shortly after the second movement began, the performance was brought to a sudden halt when a gigantic crystal chandelier weighing hundreds of pounds fell from the ceiling and crashed to the part of the floor occupied only a few minutes before by the listeners. Thereafter, Haydn's Symphony number 96 in D Major has been known as the *Miracle* Symphony.

In London, Ontario, the famous comedienne of the 1930s, Beatrice Lillie, was on stage in the Noel Coward revue, *This Year of Grace*. Ranged behind her was a long line of chorus girls, as she sang

"Britannia Rules the Waves," a number she had performed numerous times. Concluding the second verse was a cue for the chorus to move onto center stage. But for the first and only time in her long career, Miss Lillie seemed to forget her act and sang the first verse again.

The chorus could not move because of what everyone at the time assumed was a loss of memory on the part of their star. Just before completing her unscheduled repeat of the first verse, as the dancers were at last about to take their position at center stage, an enormous arc light weighing at least one hundred pounds swung wildly out of control from high overhead and crashed into fragmented glass and twisted metal precisely where the chorus girls would have been standing had not Lillie "muffed" her number. If they had taken their rehearsed position at the moment assigned to them, at least some of the dancers would have been severely injured, if not killed (Vaughn, pp. 33, 34).

Both of these similar incidents imply that altered states of consciousness brought about through the focused mental powers of artistic experience leaf over into something other than rational awareness of an invisible organizing mechanism behind our physical reality. The two spheres of existence intermesh constantly, like the grinding gears of a cosmic timepiece as large as the universe. But the relationship between the two spheres becomes apparent to us only when they connect in moments of synchronicity.

Crisis Synchronicity
Warnings

A subtle chain of countless rings
The next unto the farthest brings;
The eye reads omens where it goes,
And speaks all languages the rose.

—Ralph Waldo Emerson, *Nature*

Meaningful coincidences that warn of impending dangers are usually regarded as premonitions of misfortune only after they come to pass. The first half of a significant coincidence is difficult to identify until it has connected with its meaningful counterpart. Recognizing such a phenomenon before it is completed requires skill, which some people develop through years of blindly following each synchronicity that enters their lives. They develop an intuitive sense that they accept as a form of special guidance.

Whether premonitions foreshadow the inevitable, or, at least in some instances, represent warnings of difficulties we are able to avoid, has been debated by thinkers since ancient times. In *A*

111

Christmas Carol, when Scrooge is presented with a view of coming events, he asks, "Are these the shadows of things that may occur or of things that must be?" The Spirit of the Future makes no reply, the implication being that some part of the future is alterable and another is not. Scrooge does, after all, amend his materialistic ways and changes the previously dreadful outcome. With Scrooge's question, we enter upon the power of fate, regarded by some as inexorable, by others as amendable. The former view was held by a small minority of our study group, while most people aware of synchronicity expressed belief in the positive quality of most, if not all, premonitions to warn of impending troubles.

An illustrative example belongs to a New York secretary, Christine MacArthur, who began noticing an unusual knocking coming from under the front of her car whenever she made a left turn. The noise was not loud, nor did it sound serious. It was not even persistent but would come and go. Once, she was actually on her way to a repair shop to have her car's front end inspected, but she turned around and went home just before arriving because the noise had vanished. Days later, it started in again. The knocking was probably not important, and she balked at the prospect of an inspection that would almost certainly be a waste of money. She also realized that she had forgotten both the name and address of the shop that specialized in her model vehicle. She strained her memory, but could not remember its location. It was too trivial a concern after all.

Christine then resolved to forget the matter altogether and turned on the radio to get her mind on something else. Virtually the first words to come from the speaker were part of a commercial about the same specialty repair shop she had been trying to remember just moments earlier; its name and address were mentioned repeatedly. As though to emphasize the synchronicity, the station that happened to come on was one she listened to only rarely, and she did not recall ever having heard the repair shop advertised on the radio before. She resolved at once to have her car inspected. Mechanics found a badly damaged front axle that needed immediate replacement. Had she continued to drive on it, the entire right wheel would have fallen off. Because Christine usually drove at high speeds on the expressway, the consequences could have been disastrous.

Meaningful coincidences, particularly those that attempt to warn the participants of some impending and dangerous situation, are often fundamentally connected to family members. Another automobile-related premonition came through a triple dream synchronicity that began with a Florida woman. Julia Rockwell dreamt that her younger brother failed to reconnect a vital engine part in the stock car he was about to enter in a race. Totally ignorant of mechanics, she was nevertheless able to perfectly describe the neglected brake cable. The vivid dream concluded with Julia frantically trying, unsuccessfully, to make her warning heard above the noise of her brother's car revving its motor. While she was dreaming about the fatal rod, he dreamt that she woke him up, yelling incomprehensibly. Simultaneously, his wife had a dream that her sister-in-law's face was floating ominously over their bed. Alarmed, both the brother and his wife jumped out of bed, turned on all the lights, and searched the house. Although they found nothing wrong, they were still uneasy by early morning and telephoned the man's sister. When the brother learned of his sister's dream, he went to the garage and began inspecting his stock car. There he found a broken brake cable. Had he driven the car as intended, it would have certainly been involved in a wreck of some kind (Ryback and Sweitzer, p. 63).

In December 1985, an elderly Atlanta woman dreamt that someone broke into her sister's home and beat her with a baseball bat. In the morning, the sister telephoned to say that she had had the same dream. Acting on this coincidence, she temporarily moved out of her house, which was burglarized the following night ("Woman Saved by Dream?" p. 68).

A preponderance of synchronous warnings occur in dreams, because in waking life these warnings tend to be lost in the shuffle of daily affairs. In sleep, the mind is focused entirely on the dream. In the waking state, such impressions appear as visions that are more easily dismissed by our rational faculty as imaginative fantasies. If the dreaming premonition is vivid or powerful enough, it makes an impression that lasts into wakefulness. Most people will more readily act upon a precognitive warning received as a dream, if only because their conscious mind will have had nothing to do with it and therefore could not be accused of manufacturing a fantasy.

Death

Death is by far the most commonly reported theme of all major synchronicities. As Combs and Holland write, "no other event in human experience is associated with so rich an array of psychic phenomena as is death" (p. 22). Variations on this motif are radically diverse, indicating the great number of especially meaningful coincidences connecting, literally and physically, this life with the beyond. Premonitions of death appear to be something other than warnings; the former seem to foreshadow the inevitable, while the latter indicate coming events still within some measure of our control. The line separating the two is not always clearly defined.

But dreams are only one of numerous media used by premonition. After a New Year's Eve party, a photograph was taken of Willie, our family dog. The much-beloved pet was in perfect health. But when the photograph was developed, everything in it clearly appeared except Willie, whose position in the picture was represented by empty space resembling a shadow. The photographer, a family member, was suddenly possessed with the sad feeling that his dog would soon be dead, although there was no cause for alarm. A few days later, Willie was run over and killed by a passing car.

Some people need neither dreams nor photographs to know when death is near. Individuals with this dubious talent (known for thousands of years among various cultures, including Vedic India, Pharaonic Egypt, and many Native American tribes) claim to detect a discoloration and/or diminishment of the victim's aura, a rainbowlike energy field they believe emanates from and surrounds all organic matter.

During the summer of 1930, a boy swimming in a Wisconsin lake disappeared. He was assumed drowned, but the best efforts of legions of rescuers did not result in finding him. Not part of the search team, a pair of elderly Winnebago men in a rowboat took them to a spot where the water was particularly murky and indicated that the boy was down there. Minutes later, his lifeless body was hauled from the lake. Asked later how they knew its precise location, the Native Americans said they could "see his aura fading like the light of a firefly that just died." While this example is not precognitive, as it came after the fact, it is cited here to demonstrate the apparent connection in a meaningful coincidence in which the human aura is an indicator of death.

Some sensitives who know nothing about auras claim they sometimes see or intuit a strange, eerie light flashing over the face of someone close to dying. This usually yellowish glare has been most often reported by combat soldiers and medical personnel. Others engaged in premonitions insist they are able to detect the future in certain facial features, particularly expressions in the eyes of someone about to die. They look for a unique expression of melancholy resignation not associated with any other situation. It is a subtle shift, a kind of softening about the mouth and eyes, produced by the person's subconscious knowledge that life will soon end.

Relative health is not always important, and otherwise sound individuals who evidence this type of resigned expression are supposed to know that they will be killed by some external circumstance. While reading auras and facial expressions or seeing some kind of astral light may foretell imminent death, these alleged means of premonition are here regarded as interpretations of the workings of synchronicity. In other words, aura reading and the rest may be subconscious rationalizations belonging to a person suddenly confronted in a meaningful coincidence of trauma generated by the death experience.

The majority of death-oriented coincidences are not precognated. Very often, they cannot even be recognized by the people most directly involved, who die before any apparent connection is made. It is as though their experience were entirely for the benefit of surviving onlookers, who are often not in any way related to the situation. The following examples illustrate these synchronicities beyond the grave.

Steve Dempsey lost his mother when he was very young. While crossing a street, she was struck and killed by the hit-and-run driver of a station wagon. The boy was taken into the home of his aunt and uncle, who raised him as their own son. Grown and in his twenties, he was vacationing in a Western desert state, when, telephoning home, he learned of his uncle's death by natural causes. Some thirteen years later, again on a pleasure trip to the West, he happened to place a call to his aunt at the precise spot from which he learned of his uncle's passing, a spot to which he had not returned since. But this second call was all too similar. He was informed that his aunt had just died. Crossing the road on a neighborly mission of mercy, she was the victim of a station-wagon driver, who left the scene of the accident. What strange fate connected these two women who played major roles in his life?

When Lord Carnarvon passed away in Egypt at 2:00 A.M on April 5, 1923, he was unaware that his dog, left behind in England, died at precisely the same moment. Simultaneously, an unprecedented power failure suddenly shut off all the lights in Cairo, plunging the entire city into darkness. This triple synchronicity gave rise to worldwide speculation about a Curse of the Pharaoh, because Carnarvon had financed the excavation of King Tutankhamun's tomb. The tomb was found by Howard Carter, whose pet canary was revered by native diggers as a favorable omen responsible for the British archaeologist's success. A few days after his fabulous discovery, the bird was devoured by a cobra that had slithered into Carter's home (Vaughn, p. 115).

Both creatures had already become symbols of forces beyond their natural identities as beasts. The canary was considered a guiding spirit that led Carter to the tomb. As such, it was more than some localized Arabic superstition, but a vital archetype found in many cultures throughout the world. In the Germanic myth of Siegfried, for example, a colorful bird brings him fame and power by leading him to the riches of a cave formerly guarded by a dragon he just killed. Even more appropriately, the cobra was, of course, the emblem of the Egyptian pharaohs. This was the uraeus, or divine serpent, commonly depicted on the walls of royal tombs, signifying death for anyone who dared to enter. The snake attack on Carter's canary is all the more remarkable, because, long before 1923, cobras had become virtually extinct in Egypt and household encounters with them were rare.

On January 5, 1996, tenor Richard Versalle was alone onstage at New York's Metropolitan Opera Theater, performing in Leos Janecek's *The Makropulos Case*. In the opening scene, the sixty-three-year-old singer climbed to the top of a ladder that leaned against enormous filing cabinets lining the set from floor to ceiling. From this lofty perch, Versalle sang the line, "Too bad you only live so long," then fell to his death, the victim of a heart attack. While materialist psychologists may try to explain away this synchronicity by arguing that he succumbed to a combination of wish fulfillment and death wish (performers have long regarded expiring on stage as the ideal manner of death), students of meaningful coincidence refuse to believe Versalle waited until the most appropriate line before causing his own heart attack, just because he wanted to go out in style ("Opera Singer Dies on Stage" p. 18).

Another opera singer earlier succumbed to a similar synchronicity. The famous baritone Heinrich Schlussnuss concluded a 1952 recital by performing Franz Schubert's "At Twilight." A paean to the natural beauty of the world, its last line runs, "And this heart, before it breaks, still sips the glow and drinks light." In the evening, just after twilight, Schlussnuss went home and died of heart failure.

Less affronting to common sense than such acausal connections is an appreciation for the broader agenda of synchronicity, which looms larger still in another coincidental show-business death. In 1961, Hollywood star Natalie Wood had to perform a scene before the camera in which she portrayed a drowning woman. Days before the shoot, she confided to her director, Elia Kazan, that she was hydrophobic and especially afraid of dark water. The lake where she enacted her part, although turbid, was shallow (she was always standing on the bottom) and perfectly safe, with dozens of studio crewmen close by at all times.

Nevertheless, on the morning of her performance, Wood told Kazan she would be paralyzed with fear if she went into the water and said she doubted she could complete the scene. Couldn't they film it in a studio tank? she asked. That being impossible without expensive overruns, she agreed only after a man was placed in the water with her, just outside camera range. Her performance of a woman trying to drown herself was the most convincing of her career, perhaps because her panic was real. Afterward, the actress trembled with residual fear and laughed in relief.

Twenty-five years later, while trying to board a yacht around midnight, she panicked, missed a step, and fell into the water. People in a nearby boat heard her calling, "Somebody help me!" But they could not locate her in the darkness. Her drowned body was found next morning. While the actress' hydrophobia envisioned her form of death, more remarkable was a comparison of names in this lethal synchronicity. The title of Kazan's film in which Natalie Wood played the drowning scene was *Splendor in the Grass*; the name of the yacht from which she fell into the water was *The Splendor* (Kazan, p. 117). The owner of the boat had named it for its beautiful construction, not after the film.

Thomas Franklin, an audiophile with a large recording library, randomly selected a tape as background music as he worked around the house. The voice that came from the speaker belonged to Vincent Price, who was reading Longfellow's *Skeleton in Armor.* Since the tape had some months earlier been advanced practically to the end of the poem, Price was heard reciting only the last lines, which describe the final moments of the Viking warrior: "Thus, seamed with many scars, bursting these prison bars, up to its native stars, my soul ascended...." Franklin was surprised to read in the next morning's paper that, just about the hour he was listening to these words recited by the actor, Vincent Price had passed away.

Nor was this Franklin's only synchronicity of its kind. The following year, after returning home from work in the evening, he again randomly pulled a recording, one he had not heard for many months. It featured several routines performed by the British comedian Donald Cook. As before, the next day he learned that Cook had died around the same hour his recording was being played.

Synchronicity, like death itself, has no respect for people, and it stretches beyond Hollywood to reach the White House itself. In 1995, President Bill Clinton, meeting with a dozen Democratic political figures, began speaking off-the-cuff about Ron Brown, "the best commerce secretary in the history of the republic, certainly in this century, who has done more to create employment opportunities than any other secretary of commerce." Clinton continued to elaborate on the man's life, almost as though delivering a eulogy. "He went on for several minutes about Ron Brown's contributions," recalled Democrat Party chair Mark Andrew, who attended the small conference.

Just as it adjourned, the President was briskly ushered into the Oval Office by grim-faced party staffers, who informed him of Ron Brown's death in a plane crash. Referring to Clinton's remarks only a few minutes before learning the sad news about his esteemed commerce secretary, Andrew said, "He spoke of him in the most glowing terms and there was something prescient about it that made it very eerie" ("Andrew recalls 'Eerie' News of Brown's Death," p. 11).

Carl Jung himself was not immune to deadly synchronicities. Troubled one night for no reason he could understand, he had difficulty falling asleep. Around 2:00 A.M., he suddenly awoke with the distinct impression that someone had quickly entered his bedroom. Throwing on the light switch, he found no indication of a break-in,

although he still experienced the sensation of some nameless visi-
tation. He then realized that he had been awakened by a ferocious
headache. The pain seemed to strike him from the middle of his
forehead, coursing all the way to the back of his skull.

Eventually, the headache subsided, and he was able to return
to sleep. In the morning, he learned that one of his patients had
committed suicide by shooting himself in the forehead with a
pistol, the bullet embedding itself in the back wall of his skull. The
man had taken his life at two o'clock the previous night, just when
Jung had awakened with his headache (Bolen, pp. 33, 34).

Mortal synchronicities followed Jung beyond the grave. As the
eighty-five-year-old pioneer psychologist lay dying at his beautiful
Swiss home in Kuesnacht on June 6, 1961, a powerful thunder-
storm blew across nearby Lake Zurich. Its arrival coincided with his
passing. Not two hours later, his favorite tree, which had survived
decades of storms, was utterly demolished by lightning. Years later,
the narrator of a British television documentary was describing
Jung's death and the synchronous loss of his beloved tree. While
the narrator stood in front of the cameras, on the very premises of
Jung's Swiss home, lightning struck the same garden where the tree
had been formerly located, followed by a dramatic roll of thunder
(van der Post, p. 275).

Karma is the moral equivalent for Newton's physical law that
states, "For every action, there is an equal and opposite reaction." It
seems to circulate throughout instances of synchronicity, particularly those dealing with death. Perhaps the most illustrative
example belonged to Henry Ziegland, a Texan who, in 1893,
callously betrayed his fiancée. Overwhelmed by despair, the
woman took her own life. Her brother, seeking to avenge her
death, found Ziegland out in the open and fired a revolver at point-
blank range. His victim fell to the ground. The distraught brother
then killed himself. But Ziegland actually survived his assailant. The
intended bullet had only grazed his cheek and lodged itself in a
nearby tree. He did not accept his lucky survival graciously,
however, and over the following years continued to berate and
insult the memories of the dead woman and her would-be avenger
of a brother.

Then, in 1913, Ziegland was engaged in cutting down an old
tree. Unable to make much progress with his axe, he girdled it with
sticks of dynamite. Although at a safe distance from the explosion,

he fell dead. The coroner found a bullet had passed through his skull and determined that it was the same bullet fired at him by the irate brother of his betrothed. Ziegland had dynamited the same tree in which the lodged bullet waited for twenty years (*Ripley's Believe It or Not!*, p. 133).

"Death is not always a judgment," according to Lone Red Eagle, a Menomonie shaman renowned for his careful preservation of the ancient ways. "It is sometimes the Great Healer." A case in point belongs to Chicago housewife Virginia Hardyman. Around 5:00 A.M., she was awakened by the distinct, almost overpowering perfume of flowers filling her room. It was as if enormous bouquets had been stacked all around her bed. But there was nothing to be seen, no physical cause for so unmistakable a fragrance. She assumed it was the psychical residue of a forgotten dream, but, unable to go back to sleep, she enjoyed the sensation for several long minutes.

Later that same day, Virginia learned that her aunt died peacefully in her sleep about 5:00 A.M., just when the scent of so many flowers had filled the bedroom. Her aunt had been a second mother to her, and the two had been exceptionally close since she was a little girl. Moreover, the aunt had been an enthusiastic gardener who delighted in her summertime profusion of flowers. The woman felt a deep sense of certainty that her aunt had survived death and returned to show her liberation from earthly cares in a loving gift that simultaneously identified herself.

Rescue

While some synchronicities seem to connect inescapably with death, others make possible perfectly timed life-saving rescues. In the summer of 1995, Don Augusta had just loaded up his tanker with two hundred gallons of water. Driving on the highway, he saw a car engulfed in flames. Its twenty-year-old driver, Heather Skaggs, had fallen asleep at the wheel. Her vehicle hit two trees, rolled over, and caught fire just before the truck driver arrived. He opened the valve on his tanker and extinguished the blaze, allowing rescuers to cut Skaggs free. She was released from the hospital two days later in satisfactory condition. "It was a miracle that I had that truck of water," Augusta told a newspaper reporter ("A Watery Coincidence," p. 17).

In another synchronous highway incident, a student who had been involved all week in intensive first-aid training was annoyed when family members pressured him to attend a boring family function on his one day off. He reluctantly agreed, but left the party as early as he could. He took the expressway home, which was not his usual route.

Perhaps fifteen minutes after getting on the freeway, he saw a stopped patrol car off to the side with its emergency lights flashing. Approaching it at a decreasing speed, he noticed two badly damaged passenger vehicles stalled in the grassy median strip. Pulling over, he got out and ran to one of the smashed-up cars. Inside was a severely injured elderly man who was bleeding profusely. Remembering his training of only several days before, the first-aid student properly bound up his wounds and skillfully employed the instruments from his school kit he just happened to have brought along. The patrolman had placed a call for help, but assistance had not yet arrived. There were other crash victims at the scene, some of whom needed immediate medical attention. The student had his hands full, but he made all the right moves and was told by a paramedic who finally showed up that he undoubtedly saved the lives of several people.

The paramedic's ambulance was delayed in the traffic tie-up generated by passing motorists who slowed down to a crawl in order to gawk at the accident. It took place just before the first-aid student arrived on the scene. Had he left the party a minute or so earlier, he would have missed it entirely, and if he had arrived any later, there probably would have been some fatalities. If he had not gone to the party at all, as was his original inclination, the victims would have suffered unaided too long.

In July 1990, Weston Kilpatrick was born with a life-threatening heart condition. He suffered from terminal aortic and valve defects, with holes between the right and left ventricles. His heart was beyond repair, and a suitable donor had to be found if the infant was to survive. Weston's parents prayed night and day for their imperiled son, and he became the entire focus of their lives. Eventually, the doctors could do nothing more for the child. Then, fifteen months after his birth and one day before they determined that his heart was failing, a donor was found. Weston survived to become a normal, healthy boy (Tevas, p. 19).

The perfect timing of such arrivals by the right person at the right place is commonly regarded as providential. An illustrative example concerns a woman with no medical background who dreamed she was floating high over the city in which she lived. From her aerial vantage point, she could see all the city's residents and their activities, as well as all the businesses. She even saw herself walking to lunch. Then her attention focused on a man with large, horn-rimmed glasses, wearing a black coat and carrying a dilapidated brown briefcase. She knew he was very sick with nausea and chest pains, frightened, and unable to breathe, because she felt every detail of his distress. He collapsed in the street; she suddenly descended into her physical body and ran over to assist him.

Walking to work the next morning, she noticed the man in her dream, down to his black coat, eyeglasses, and battered brown briefcase. Astounded, she saw him stagger and fall just as she had envisioned. She ran over to him. Because she understood precisely what was wrong with him, she was able to describe his condition in such detail over the telephone to rescue workers that they knew just how to save his life. At the hospital, the accuracy of her on-the-spot diagnosis was confirmed, and the man responded to treatment (Ryback, p. 67).

Parapsychologists might interpret the woman's apparently pre-cognitive dream as an instance of astral projection, in which the soul, temporarily liberated from its bodily home, either in sleep or some other altered state of consciousness (as from narcotics, illness, or ritual), freely roams across the boundaries of space and time, actually visiting what to us is the future, and returning to our present dimension with important information. This is exactly what the shaman in tribal societies is required to perform on behalf of his or her people. While, in the foregoing case, astral projection might indeed have been the mechanism by which her providential meeting with a heart-attack victim came about, it is not likely to have been the cause of that connection between the dreamer and its object. The woman in question recalled no other dreams, either before or since, in which she seemed to be floating above the world on astral rescue missions.

The connecting principle at work in all of the cases I've described seems to have been the power of the event itself. In looking to astral projection or telepathy for explanations of synchronicity, we are confusing causes with means. Because neither of these two phenomena satisfy universal understanding of meaningful coincidences, we must regard them as merely the connecting methods for synchronous events.

A famous case of mass synchronicity utterly ruled out any possible involvement by astral projection or telepathy. Fifteen choir members all agreed to meet for practice at a church on March 1, 1950, at 7:20 P.M. It was their usual place and time, and everyone always arrived promptly. Yet, on this night, unlike any other, all fifteen members were delayed for a variety of trivial causes. The minister and his family were late because his wife was still ironing their daughter's dress; a student hastened to finish her geometry homework before leaving; somebody else's car would not start; two friends wanted to hear the end of a radio show; a girl overslept her nap, delaying her and her mother by a few minutes; and so forth.

All of the delays were trifling, but they cumulatively amounted to a unique coincidence that prevented any choir member from reaching the church at the appointed time. At 7:25 P.M., the church was totally destroyed by a terrific blast when the gas furnace exploded. Had the fifteen people been assembled inside at the usual hour, as had been their custom, it is difficult to imagine how any of them could have survived (Weaver, p. 280).

This incident, perhaps to a greater extent than similar examples, demonstrates that synchronicity has no preferences. It connects just as effectively to save lives as to take them. The only differentiating factor appears to be in the timing. Perhaps there *is* "a time to live and a time to die," just as stated in the Old Testament.

Reincarnation

Although the idea of reincarnation is still generally met with skepticism outside of Asia, it is becoming increasingly accepted throughout the West, and not entirely via Eastern influences. The belief that the soul is imperishable and continually reborn through successive lifetimes has roots in the mystery cults of classical times

and even early Bronze Age religions. Yet more ancient was Neolithic
Europe's agrarian spirituality, which fitted human destiny into the
recurring cycles of seasonal change. The people of that time believed
that nature was born at the vernal equinox, matured through
summer, declined with autumn, died in winter, and returned each
spring. Humankind, being but one of nature's myriad creations, was
regarded as no less part of life's eternal process of renewal.

In this view, existence itself is analogous to our waking state,
wherein we go about our daily affairs, eventually grow tired, lie
down to sleep, dream, and awaken each morning. So too, our
conscious lives are spent in earthly activity; we grow weary with age
and lie down to die. Our soul journeys into an Otherworld, just as
our subconscious enters the realm of dreams, from which we awake
in another life. In other words, death is a dream we pass through
into a new consciousness. And both the dream state, that dimension
between one wakeful state and the next, and death, which bridges
one life with a subsequent life, are not easily remembered.

Synchronicity is playing a developing role in the growing
recognition of reincarnation, because of meaningful connections
allegedly linking present with past lives. How many of these connections are the dross of delusion or immature wish fulfillment, no
one knows. As does any previously esoteric idea that attains some
measure of popularity, it becomes vulgarized and debased in the
hands of some people—in this case, those who like to flatter themselves that they're the latest reincarnation of some great, historical
individual. Such modern-day foolishness, however, helps us to
understand and perhaps even sympathize with the ancient world
initiates of certain mystery schools, who refused to parade their
refined spiritual concepts in public and in fact cloaked them in
secrecy upon pain of death. But for all of today's past-life enthu-
siasts who enjoy believing they used to be Cleopatra or Louis XIV,
some cases give the honest investigator pause for serious reconsid-
eration, especially those in which meaningful coincidences play
important roles.

A term used to describe reincarnation, or, more properly, the
transmigration of souls, is palingenesis, from the Greek *palin*
("again") and genesis, which means beginning. Interestingly, the
term has for centuries been employed by Christian faiths to signify
baptism, that "second birth" of the soul into the Church. In biology,

palingenesis describes the development of an individual organism that reproduces the features of its ancestors. For example, you may bear little or no physical resemblance to your mother and father, but may share many more characteristics with your grandfather or an even more remote ancestor, because sets of genes sometimes skip a generation or more.

These esoteric religious and scientific definitions for the same term are different, yet nonexclusive and complementary, viewpoints of the same phenomenon. They depict the spark of life jumping the gap of death to achieve rebirth in both the spiritual and the natural world. If palingenesis is a fundamental process of existence, after all, then it manifests itself in the meaningful coincidences we experience, the synchronous connections from life to life.

Until only a few years ago, mere mention of reincarnation was condemned by scientists in the West as nothing more than late-twentieth-century superstition and New Age flummery. But a new generation of thinkers, many among the best minds of our time, has come to seriously reconsider the nature of the human soul and its role in the cycles of nature. No less a world-class scientist than Stephen Hawking went on national television to offer reincarnation as a distinct possibility because of a coincidence that has haunted his life since childhood. While just a grammar school student, he learned that Galileo Galilei, the great Italian mathematician, astronomer, and physicist, died on January 8, 1642, three hundred years to the day before Hawking was born. Did, as Hawking suggest, the soul of Galileo reincarnate in the modern American scientist?

One of the best-documented examples of reincarnation was presented in 1996 by Dr. Bruce Goldberg, a counseling psychologist in Woodland Hills, California. By chance, he separately interviewed two men who told him they experienced particularly vivid past-life recall. The first man Dr. Goldberg heard from was Arnold, who remembered being an apprentice metal worker in early-twelfth-century Europe. His name was Thayer then, and he was tyrannized by the master craftsman. Only a few years into his apprenticeship, the two got into a quarrel that escalated into a terrible fight. Thayer was killed, stabbed to death in the stomach.

A year and a half after Dr. Goldberg stopped treating Arnold, he met Brian, who wanted to understand his compulsion to manip-

126 Synchronicity & You

ulate others. Under hypnosis therapy, Brian recalled being a master metal worker in Europe in 1130 A.D. He was known then as Gustave and had taken on a new apprentice, an incompetent, it later turned out. Brian-Gustave said that the young man's name was Thayer. Two years later, they got into a serious argument that degenerated into a physical struggle, when the master tried to chain his apprentice's leg to the work table. They came to blows and Gustave admitted he'd stabbed Thayer to death in his neck and stomach (Goldberg, p. 12).

Arnold and Brian never met, nor did they ever learn of each other's past-life recall. Dr. Goldberg alone was aware of their significant relationship. He was the connecting factor in a meaningful coincidence that could not have otherwise occurred. Although the two past lives achieved a kind of credibility through Dr. Goldberg, it was actually synchronicity itself that was the overriding phenomenon. Even something as controversial and spiritual as reincarnation appears in this instance to have been essentially no different than elements in any of our previously described cases, in which telepathy, warnings, premonitions, and all the rest were subordinate to the larger issue of meaningful coincidence.

chapter 7

Synchronicity as Guidance and Destiny

The visible creation is the terminus or the circumference of the invisible world.

　　　　　　　　—Ralph Waldo Emerson, *Nature*

Many people who continually experience meaningful coincidences and acknowledge them believe that synchronicity in all its forms is a kind of personal guidance. As I've mentioned, the categories set out in these chapters to define various types of significant, acausal events often overflow their set boundaries, spilling into other classifications, merging with their definitions, and blurring precise distinctions. Nevertheless, some meaningful coincidences, like those described in this chapter, clearly offer specific guidance, sometimes almost amounting to instructions, but more commonly showing alternatives to problems otherwise not apparent.

These instances of Otherworldly direction are paths our lives take into the future, if we choose to follow them, and are, therefore, the means by which our personal destinies evolve.

Individuals who accept such life-guiding synchronicities embrace "the authentic life," as Joseph Campbell defined it—following our own truth, regardless of the consequences. This is the high destiny that the ancient Greeks called *moira* and that, they believed, is offered to every human.

Certainly, in more than a general sense, all synchronicities, because they comment so personally on our lives, are indeed signs guiding us to follow a particular direction, if only we first win the approval of our apprehensive, rational mind or courageously defy it. Here, I define guidance as those meaningful coincidences that point in a specific direction at the most opportune moment. But in our attempt to bring some clarity to an infinitely complex phenomenon that has puzzled human beings for thousands of years, we need to get a handle on so broad a subject by focusing on its individual aspects.

Guidance

One New Year's Eve, Colin McDonald was sourly reviewing all the inequities and bad breaks that had beset him the previous twelve months. "Life stinks!" he concluded in front of his wife. Attending a party later that evening, he was presented with a gift by a friend who was unaware of his negative sentiments. It was a book entitled *Life Stinks*, a comical critique of optimism. The coincidence so struck the man, who had a naturally wry sense of humor, that he found amusement in his own depression and began to take himself less seriously.

Mike Sawinski, an investor, was driving alone cross-country for five hours while thinking intensely about a cave some acquaintances claimed, with only inconclusive evidence, contained a great deal of gold. He was unsure whether or not he should become personally involved in their dubious if tempting venture. In the middle of his thoughts, half-consciously, he turned on the radio. It picked up a small station with which he was unfamiliar that was broadcasting a rare, old hit from 1937, years before he was born. Although the would-be investor had never heard the song, he was surprised when the first lyrics that came from the speaker were, "There's a gold mine in the sky."

Somewhat amazed by such appropriate words, he decided to follow the song's advice. To him it meant that the investment he was considering was just "a gold mine in the sky," a fantasy. Sawinski chose not to associate himself with the cave project, and the other investors lost heavily in their quest for the gold, which they never found.

While visiting a friend, Richard Kidolis caught sight of himself in a full-length mirror and was appalled to see how overweight he had become. Until then, he had not realized the extent of his out-of-shape condition. Imagining all the hard dieting and exercise his body obviously needed, he began to despair of ever shedding his accumulated pounds. He felt he was lazy by nature and lacked sufficient will power to apply himself to any physical regimen.

Walking into the living room, Kidolis sat down at a coffee table piled with magazines. On top was a copy of the latest issue of *Psychology Today*, its cover emblazoned with the title of a leading article: "Looking at the Man in the Mirror." He felt as though he had been instructed by some guiding force he could not understand to reconsider the overweight image of himself he'd confronted moments before in the adjacent room. That very day, he began exercising and dieting at his own pace. Gaining a new sense of self-respect in the process, he improved his general health and, before the end of the year, Kidolis had lost all his excess weight and put himself into fine shape.

Marcus Bach, author of *The World of Serendipity*, related how he was impatient to place a call while between flights one morning at the St. Louis airport. But the only remaining telephone booth was practically barred by the long legs of a clumsy stranger half sprawled across the narrow door. Stumbling over the inconsiderate lout, he felt himself becoming angrier by the moment and was on the verge of uttering a few choice words, when he recognized the man. He was a former student who had once told Bach that he admired him for his even temper (p. 80).

These cases are simple examples of the kind of subtle, albeit well-timed, guidance synchronicity provides in our daily affairs.

Such meaningful coincidences seem to nudge us in the proper direction, sometimes calling attention to our problems or short-comings more effectively than any other external influence.

Moira

The ancient Greeks believed that everyone is born with a lower and a higher destiny. The former is a human being's fate, the inescapable components in life necessary for existence—for example, one's birth, schooling, job, car, mate, offspring, and friends. Higher destiny means not doing what one was expected to do (by society, peers, or religion), but following instead the dictates of one's own heart. Such an atypical course often meant (and still means) facing the resentment of others, condemnation as a social rebel, and even perhaps financial failure.

The great American mythologist Joseph Campbell said such individuals have embarked on "the hero's journey." They live according to their own values, which share little or nothing in common with popular values. They "follow their bliss," or *moira*, a term the Greeks used to define this higher destiny. Following moira means doing what one feels most inwardly qualified and inclined to do, regardless of the social or material consequences, favorable or unfavorable.

A classic case of synchronicity expressed through moira occurred in the early life of the Buddha, before he evolved his own teachings. In these youthful years, he had already gone from self-indulgent materialism as the son of a wealthy father to the other extreme of self-denial. But even while undertaking a strenuous regimen of abnegation, he wondered if denying one's body to the point of starvation and sickness was what a loving God really expected of His own creatures. One day, while sitting by the side of a road, weak from the rigors of a prolonged fast, he saw a troop of public performers pass by. While the others danced and played their musical instruments, the Buddha listened to the song of a female vocalist: "Only when the sitar's tuned properly can we dance. Don't tune the sitar too high or low, and we will dance off with the hearts of men. An overstretched string will break and the music withers away. It dies when the string is silent because it is slack. Don't tune the sitar too high or low!" (Jacoby, p. 263).

The lyrics perfectly expressed the Buddha's thoughts at the moment, a meaningful coincidence he accepted as a providential sign. Thus encouraged, he threw off the unhealthy extremes of asceticism and began to understand that moderation in all things, even spiritual matters, was the proper path to follow. From his enlightening synchronicity at the side of the road, he eventually evolved his doctrine of the "middle path."

Following a vocation, that inner call, is not self-indulgence or an excuse for laziness. Doing what one really wants to do is hard work, but it is self-fulfilling as nothing else can be. It is the ultimate key to personal happiness in the physical world. "To be so busy," George Bernard Shaw wrote, "doing something you like, you do not have time to realize if you're happy or not—that is my definition of happiness" (Radio Broadcasts of George Bernard Shaw, p. 84).

Most people spend their lives in jobs they either hate or tolerate. At best, people in the latter category convince themselves that they enjoy work by emphasizing the positive details of their employment. Sensible people make the best of their situation and look for the bright side of life. They are fulfilling, perhaps out of pressing family necessity, their lower destiny. Perhaps it is better for civilization that they do. If everyone "followed their bliss," the world might be given over to chaos. Or, it might emerge as an entirely different world whose inhabitants live, again in Campbell's words, more "authentic lives."

Two men work side by side as street sweepers. One hates the job, which he took on only because nothing else was available, while the other feels entirely fulfilled, because he truly enjoys the work more than anything else he can imagine. The former is pursuing his fate; the latter, his moira.

The difference between these two kinds of destiny was dramatically presented in the 1968 Stanley Kubrick motion picture, *2001: A Space Odyssey*. At the end of the film, as the consequence of a failed mission to the planet Jupiter resulting in the death of everyone on board the spaceship, an astronaut is sent careening toward irretrievable oblivion at immeasurable speeds across space and time. He suddenly sees himself back on Earth as an old man living in soft, luxurious accommodations and richly attired, sitting alone at a table and eating a fine meal. Reaching for something, he accidentally knocks over a glass of wine, which shatters and spills on the floor. The old man slowly bends down, sadly staring at the broken crystal fragments, the scarlet pool, then looks up meaningfully at himself as a younger man standing before him in his space suit.

The broken glass and spilled wine are classic metaphors for a wasted life. The astronaut sees what would have become of himself had he not gone on the Jupiter mission. He would have lived a long, safe, prosperous, prosaic, unauthentic life. Instead, he chose to follow his bliss along the hero's journey to fulfill the dictates of his heart. He made a decision for the quality of his years, not their quantity.

In 1336, the greatest scholar of his age, Petrarch, climbed to the top of Italy's Mount Ventoux. He needed temporary escape from the distraction of society and wanted to clear his thoughts for the great task that lay before him, which turned out to be launching the European Renaissance. Reaching the summit, he admired the stunningly beautiful view of the world below, then randomly opened the single book he'd brought along, Saint Augustine's *Confessions*, and read these words: "And men go abroad to admire the heights of mountains, the mighty billows of the sea, the broad tide of rivers, the compass of the ocean, and the circuits of the stars, and pass themselves by" (Hillman, pp. 195, 196).

The connection of this excerpt with his visit to the mountaintop produced so powerful an effect on Petrarch that, as Grasse wrote, he "was catalyzed into a process of introspection and transformation that led to his influential writings, pointed to by some as a symbolic starting point for Renaissance thought" (Grasse, p. 37).

But if fate is imposed on us, moira is voluntary. We are driven to do the things we must by desires, inborn or acquired, and forced into certain behavior by necessity. Moira is something offered to us, a chance to rise above mere survival and the transient values of others, to be true to the best in our inner self. It is our real work, whether that be running a billion-dollar corporation or tending a home garden. What all this has to do with synchronicity will become apparent in the following cases. Their meaningful coincidences light the way from our lower to our higher destinies. They also confirm that the activity in which we are engaged does indeed belong to our moira, thus reassuring us that we are on the proper path toward living the authentic life, being true to ourselves.

Jung experienced a decisive moira synchronicity during the most crucial period of his life and career, sixteen years after his break with Sigmund Freud, his former idol and mentor. Since then, the younger man had received no support for his unconventional ideas. He was in an intellectual and emotional limbo, trying to systematize his thoughts by writing a new book. *Memories, Dreams and Reflections* was a radical departure from mainline psychology, and Jung was wracked with self-doubt and fearful of the inevitably savage response from his influential critics. His preoccupation with new ideas had cost him his comfortable university tenure and isolated him from most of his colleagues. He was pursuing the lonely path of the hero's journey, and now, after so many years of apparent failure to have his theories taken seriously, he wondered if he had made the right decision after all.

During this time of internal turmoil, Jung had the particularly vivid dream of a golden castle. So brilliant was its persistent image that he began painting it from memory at the center of a mandala (Sanskrit for a "circular design" used in meditation). As the painting progressed, it took on a Chinese aspect. He was in the process of finishing it when he received an advance copy of *The Secret of the Golden Flower*. Its author, Richard Wilhelm, had for the first time translated from the Chinese this one-thousand-year-old text "on the yellow castle," which paralleled and confirmed the very ideas Jung was just then agonizing over.

The effect of this meaningful coincidence was to restore Jung's confidence in his work and himself. It acted as a needful reassurance that the solitary way he'd chosen was the right road to his higher destiny. He followed it the rest of his life to become one of the most influential thinkers of the twentieth century. Had he ignored his moira and returned to that cushy job as a teacher and lecturer who subordinated his own truth in order to avoid offending other people, he would have died without making a larger contribution to civilization.

A precursor of Jung's investigation into synchronicity was the astronomer Camille Flammarion. He was among the first scientists to research meaningful coincidences and their relationship to death and dying. Flammarion experienced his own significant acausality while writing *The Unknown*, which departed from strongly held conceptions about the nature of Earth's atmosphere. Eventually realizing that the ideas he suggested were diametrically opposed to contemporary opinion, he hesitated in the middle of writing a chapter about the nature of wind. Just then, a terrific gust of wind gathered up all the papers he had been working on and swept them through an open window. Flammarion ran outside and spent hours tracking down every one. Returning to his apartment with his crumpled collection, he concluded that he had been chastised for doubting his course because of what others might think of him. He resumed his work, which laid the basis for modern meteorology.

Even highly successful novelists like Rebecca West have their moments of doubt. After she had spent what she considered too many months laboring on a new book, her self-confidence began to wane and she wondered, as does every author at some time in his or her career, if she had written herself out. She put down her pen after having just written about a girl finding a hedgehog in her garden. The very idea seemed silly and she was about to scratch out the passage, when she was interrupted by a female servant who asked West to come see a hedgehog the woman had just found in the garden. Dame Rebecca kept all references to hedgehogs, finished her novel in record time, and saw *Harriet Hume* become an outstanding success.

Few motion pictures were more plagued with production nightmares than the 1939 version of *The Wizard of Oz*. Among the lesser, although vexing, problems confronting Victor Fleming (one of five directors associated with the film) was something as simple as locating the right kind of coat for the traveling fortune-teller to wear. Incredibly, the studio did not possess a single frock coat that fit Frank Morgan, who portrayed Professor Marvel, or satisfied Fleming. He gave an ultimatum to the head of the props department, saying, "Bring me the coat I want after lunch, or you're fired!" Production had already gone far over budget, so falling behind now on its shooting schedule would result in the film's cancellation. In a panic, the props chief ran from the lot and sprinted several miles to the nearest pawn shop. There, in the back room, he found an old black coat he hoped would pacify the director. It looked about the right size, too. He returned in time for the shoot to find that the long-tailed coat fit actor Morgan perfectly and met Fleming's specifications.

Months later, after filming and editing were completed and all the props were collected and returned to storage, the coat used for Professor Marvel's part hit a bureaucratic snag. The item was not in the Warner Brothers stock catalogue, and the prop chief had to explain how and where he obtained it. Turning the collar up to sew in a company label, he was surprised to find a tag bearing the name of its former owner. It read simply, "L. Frank Baum," author of the original *Wizard of Oz* series of children's books. Baum had already been dead for twenty years, so he could not appreciate this meaningful coincidence, made all the more intriguing because he personally identified with the character who wore the coat, Professor Marvel. The connection was appropriate, nevertheless, in that the 1939 film version did more to popularize his life's work than any publishing effort could have.

Another piece of moira that went unnoticed by the person whom it most concerned involved Wolfgang Pauli, one of the modern world's most important physicists and Jung's colleague in early research of significant acausality. When Pauli died on December 15, 1958, a young, unknown student was taking a university examination in Liverpool, England. F. David Peat was surprised to read an exam question that asked how the nature of the universe would have been perceived had Pauli's exclusion principle never existed. The irony of the coincidence affected Peat so deeply that he devoted his life to investigating the subject, eventually publishing something of a classic in the field, *Synchronicity: The Bridge Between Matter and Mind*.

School exams often spark synchronicities connecting students, who are intensely involved and focused on their tests, to their moira. A college senior taking her finals dreamed of a biology examination scheduled in the morning. She envisioned its third page, which featured a diagram with related questions. Awakening from her dream, she was curious to know if such a diagram actually existed. Flipping through her biology textbook, she found it exactly as it appeared in her subconscious mind and hurriedly memorized everything connected with the illustration. When taking her exam a few hours later, she turned immediately to the third page and found the same diagram and associated material that had appeared in her dream the night before. After graduating, she went on to become a professional in several fields related to biology.

For many people who give up the security of lower destiny to follow their moira, their time is more valuable than any monetary compensation. They believe that working for others, if the tasks involved are not compatible with their own inner truth, is to place a wholly insufficient monetary value on their lives. When we barter ourselves for the fulfillment of someone else's truth we always come up short-changed, no matter how great the material compensation. We sacrifice that which we really most want to achieve because of others' expectations. Only so many breaths are allowed us from the moment we are born until we die. To squander them on something we cannot call our own is to waste our natural inheritance, the most precious commodity we possess—time. It is therefore better to fail in the pursuit of our real work than to succeed at anything that is not; success in the latter would actually be a betrayal of our own truth, while merely to pursue the former is to successfully live the authentic life. Moreover, we abrogate our inner genuineness when we accept others' notions of what is successful or not. To follow our higher destiny, we must have the strength and courage be true to ourselves.

Men and women who steer the course of their lives by such bold viewpoints travel the hero's journey. To them, it is less important that some heroes meet tragic ends than that they used their time heroically. Life's real value, they insist, may be found only in the quest for one's own truth, regardless of the outcome.

Stephen Diamond certainly followed his own lights, regardless of the opinions of society. But instead of seeking his higher destiny, he indulged himself in pointless and destructive self-gratification. With only $10 to his name, he arrived in San Francisco, where he experienced the recurrent effects of the mescaline he had taken in the recent past. He was soon utterly penniless, but he felt a nervous desire to write down everything he was feeling. Now, unable to afford even the cheapest notepad, he resolved to shoplift one from a local drugstore. But once there, his good conscience got the better of him and he found himself on the sidewalk again, emotionally worse off than before, but still burning to commit his sensations to writing. Just then, he noticed "a pad of paper, face-down on top of a pile of rubbish, clothes, shoes, old books." It was a beautiful medical tablet that had about two hundred clean sheets with a name printed in capital letters at the top of each one: "STEPHEN DIAMOND, M.D." It was his own name. This double dose of synchronicity had so profound an effect on him that he turned his life around, eventually writing a best-seller, *What the Trees Said*. Diamond was, indeed, his own best doctor (Vaughn, pp. 80, 81).

To demonstrate that moira coincidences are not flukes of chance or once-in-a-lifetime probabilities, the following examples are taken from my own synchronicity journal over a twelve-month period. During that time, I was deeply engaged in completing several books, one about Atlantis, which I had been researching and writing for the previous sixteen years.

January 23: Finally got around to reading, several years after obtaining it, an obscure paper about the Atlantis legend. Perhaps several dozen copies were printed by an even more obscure group, calling itself The International Guild of Sorcerers. I have never heard of this organization before, nor had any contact with its followers. While in the midst of studying the manuscript for the first time, I received a telephone call from a man who shared with me some of his unique, although not entirely incredible, notions regarding Egypt's Great Pyramid, ideas that tended to confirm some of my own conclusions. In the course of his conversation, he asked me, 'Have you ever heard of The International Guild of Sorcerers?' and subsequently identified himself as a member.

February 2: On an impulse, I telephoned Joe, a friend, whom I had not spoken with for the last several months. In the course of our conversation, I brought up the name of a respected researcher in Mesoamerican cosmology, Bruce Scofield. Joe was surprised because, not five minutes before I called, he read of Scofield for the first time and was wondering where to find his book, which was only published in a limited edition. He also wanted to contact the author, but could not imagine how he could reach him. As it turned out, I have not only a copy of the same title but Scofield's mailing address, both of which I sent to Joe, who is conducting some important historical research.

March 1: While working on the author section, I cut out Edna Ryneveld's biography for inclusion in a new arrangement I was putting together. We have been out of touch with each other for about a year now. As I put her information aside, the telephone rang. It was Edna. She called to tell me about some synchronicity involving my current feature article in *Fate*. She did not even realize I wrote it until I told her. She had been flipping through the magazine from back to front and happened to stop at the part that describes how the sun is aligned with the apex of Chephren's Pyramid in Egypt at the vernal equinox. Just then, she looked up at a stained-glass window in the image of a pyramid with the sun poised at its apex. Edna happened to be sitting under this unusual design while browsing through *Fate*. She went on to say that it was a gift from its creator, a friend, who could not explain why she had given it, but had decided to proceed on some nameless impulse.

May 14: After enthusing to a friend about the chapter in my book describing the internal mystery of Egypt's Great Pyramid, I happened to look over at his brother, who was playing with an unusual toy. It was a transparent plastic pyramid, at the very center of which was a puzzle of several movable pieces.

July 8th: I was writing about a speech given to his fellow World War I pilots by a Captain Bowen, then broke off to find some background information from among the stack of related books recently checked out from the local public library. Finding just the right material, I turned the book over on its spine to learn that the author's name was "Bowen," no relation to the U.S. Army Air Corps captain. Only a few minutes later, I was writing about Bowen's crew members assembling for their first group photograph. At that moment, my publisher walked into my office to tell me, "You'd better take care of this," handing me a copy of the very photo I was in the process of describing.

September 15: This morning, while driving over a bridge that crossed the freeway, I was listening to a radio broadcast in which the announcer was reading the last lines from Matthew XIII in the New Testament. Much later, in the evening, I was on my way to deliver a talk about Atlantis at the local chapter of the Edgar Cayce

Organization. A few minutes before arriving at the lecture hall, I found myself crossing the same bridge over the freeway. The radio was on again, and the program I heard earlier in the day was being rebroadcast. Just as I crossed the bridge, the line from Matthew XIII was spoken once more: "A prophet is not without honor, save in his own country and in his own house." Edgar Cayce, who was much criticized during his life as a psychic healer, was known as "the Sleeping Prophet."

October 12th: I just finished writing the latest chapter, titled "Where is Atlantis?," when I was invited to participate in a game of Trivial Pursuit. I virtually never play cards, but tonight I indulged myself in order to relax. Some time into the game, I pulled a card that read, "Name the supposed location of Atlantis."

These incidents represent a fraction of all the meaningful coincidences I recorded within the parameters of a single year. I've cited them here because they fall into the moira category and show that such synchronous events are not rare, disconnected episodes. Instead, they go beyond themselves to form meaningful patterns and even a wider series of interrelating connections between individual human beings and their true paths in life. Seen in the aggregate, they form a kind of subtle guidance nudging us in the direction of our higher selves. They direct us along a nobler path toward our moira, the hero's journey each one of us may take in our quest for the authentic life.

chapter **8**

The Transformational Experience

Can such things be, and overcome us like a summer's cloud, without our special wonder?
—William Shakespeare, *Macbeth*, Act III, Scene iv

Some meaningful coincidences are so extraordinary that they exert major shifts in an individual's psychological condition. They are genuinely life-changing, traumatically well-timed links between one's inner crisis and outer, apparently unconnected surroundings and events. Dramatic incidents of this kind are transformational experiences that permanently alter our views and attitudes. They are profoundly revealing flashes of self-recognition, which, once beheld, make an indelible impression on our personality. The transformational experience parallels that elusive, crucial moment in alchemy when one metal was changed into another. Not everyone is subjected to a single acausal event so powerful it modifies their very existence. What distinguishes this particular classification from the rest is the magnitude of its effect, as perceived by the individual connected to it, and its power to convert a personally important aspect of one's life from one condition into another.

The following example was related by Dennis Wright, a painter in my research group. While it has a Christian spin, the particular denomination of the person experiencing a synchronicity is as incidental to its final impression as any of its other transitory elements. Wright was raised in the Catholic Church, surrounded all his life by the traditional symbols that stood for and gave expression to his spiritual needs. Consequently, the transformational experience spoke to him in the kind of symbolic language that he could not only understand, but also take to heart.

As a student in the middle of his college years, Wright was under heavy parental pressure to abandon his studies in graphic art. His heart's desire had always been to become a professional painter, a vocation at extreme odds with the desires of his father, who had other, more lucrative plans for his son. If he pursued his education, he was sure to be disinherited, which would mean a substantial material loss, though one that was still not as great as losing the emotional support of his family. The only alternative was to comply with his father's wishes and abandon his desired career. Following his bliss could only be purchased with the loss of lifelong security. Moreover, his father had given him an ultimatum, so a decision was expected.

To complicate his difficulties, the young man had for the last several months been going through a difficult personal period of the type known in the Catholic Church as "the dark night of the soul." This phrase refers to a not uncommon condition of doubt experienced by otherwise devout people who feel their prayers are not being heard. Their faith seems to be melting away, and they find belief in spiritual values increasingly difficult to maintain. Sometimes, they feel shut out by God, with whom they grow angry. It was this spiritual abandonment the student was undergoing just when he received his father's "last word." While not a particularly religious follower of the Church, the young man had maintained his Catholic faith since childhood, at least until "the dark night of the soul" came over him. No doubt, the spiritual and paternal crises were reflections of each other, representing both ends of the same psychological dilemma.

But now things had come to a head, and he found himself suddenly impatient not only with his father but also with God. One seemed very much like a reflection of the other. In an effort to clear his mind, he walked to a nearby park and found a lonely bench, where he tried to sort out his teeming thoughts. The place was virtually abandoned, save for a few small children playing nearby and one or two other solitary figures like himself shuffling in the distance among the trees. Suddenly, all the frustration seething in him over the last several months reached a boiling point. He silently, though passionately, delivered his last prayer, more of an ultimatum to God than a prayer:

"Look, I've prayed to you for help with this problem a thousand times, but you just ignore me. All I'm asking for is guidance, some direction. I want to know which way to go. I've explained my problem to you over and over again until I just don't think you're even around to hear me, or anybody else, for that matter. If I were trying to telephone somebody like you, I would have given up long before today. You're supposed to be omnipotent, but with all your power you can't even stoop to assist just one of your creatures with the crisis of his life. I am this close to chucking any belief in you at all. I'll never bother to call on you again, for anything, because I'm not so sure anymore you even exist. If you do, you're not much help, so I'll rely on myself from now on. I'm beginning to feel ashamed of myself for even thinking you might hear me. Here's the deal: Give me tangible, material proof that you really exist, or you'll never hear from me again. Either you show yourself, right now, materialize here, in front of me, at this moment, or it's quits!"

Precisely at that moment, a dirty little girl ran up to him, a total stranger, demanding, "Here, Mister, look at this!" as she brandished a small plastic crucifix a few inches from his face.

He laughed out loud, frightening the child, and she ran away, the cheap crucifix still clutched in her hand. She could have never guessed that her synchronous appearance that spring afternoon had been for him a transformational experience of the first order. In a single moment, his long-lingering "dark night of the soul" was dispelled and his faith restored. He felt relieved, unburdened of more than a religious crisis. Clarity seemed to filter through his mind like a dried-up sponge soaking up clear water. His nerves grew calm. They relaxed in a kind of spiritual certainty he had never known before. He felt a tangible connection leading from the innermost part of himself to something beyond reason. And from his sense of renewal and well-being emerged a determination to follow his heart's desire, to become an artist.

But even the shedding of new light on his path through life was entirely secondary to the awe that descended over him. He had been ushered into a veritable holy-of-holies and experienced a personalized mysticism beyond sharing with anyone else. Something valuable had been added to his life that no one could ever take from him.

Another transformational coincidence that demonstrated its magical power as a life-changing experience took place near a small town three hundred miles south of Lima, where Philip Vanderdecken, an American tourist, had come to witness the astronomical event of the year. Early in 1994, he learned that a total eclipse of the sun would occur on his birthday. But the celestial event could be seen only within a narrow band across the middle of South America, preferably someplace in the south of Peru. As much as he wanted to celebrate himself in this unique way, the best round-trip airfare to South America his travel agent could find for him cost $1,200, far beyond his means. He resigned himself to the fact that his next birthday would have to pass without any astronomical extravaganza.

A few days after his travel agent gave him the bad news about his airline ticket, Vanderdecken received an unexpected commission for a side job that required little work. He was offered exactly $1,200. Taking his fee as "a sign from somebody that I'm supposed to celebrate my birthday in Peru," he eagerly made plans for a special birthday. Arriving in Lima a week before the eclipse, he took a bus to the town of Nazca, where people from all over the world were gathering to witness the event. Up until a day or two before it was to take place, he enjoyed his time in Peru immensely.

But as the hours till his birthday grew short, his spirits were progressively overtaken by a deepening melancholy. Leaving his hotel one morning, Philip wandered out of town toward the desert, away from the sea, toward the mountains. There he climbed one to its summit, from which he saw nothing but arid rock and sand in all directions, spreading to the horizon. Even at this altitude, he could not shake a deepening sense of despair, a feeling of remorse for a life of missed opportunities and unfulfilled hopes. From his high perspective, he seemed to have a clear view of the long roll of years that led up to the present moment. Vanderdecken began recalling all his miscalculations and botched efforts, going back even into his childhood. He catalogued all his recollected failures and defeats. He gave himself no passing grades in any aspect of his life. His chosen career had fizzled out, and his personal affairs without exception ended in emotional shipwreck. It was fitting he had come to Peru for an eclipse, because the very word meant "failure." So too, his life had been eclipsed by too many years of disappointed hopes, rendering it without merit. His sense of self-worth had never fallen so low. Even his will to live seemed less strong, and he speculated that dying of starvation alone on top of this mountain might not be such a terrible fate. He had had fits of depression before, but never as deep as this.

Thinking he was alone, he was surprised to suddenly notice another man, perhaps three hundred feet away, standing motionless at the edge of a crag. Staring at him, he saw that the stranger was weeping silently. The muted sound of a distant bell then echoed through the valley far below, and he could make out a procession of native people winding their way to the small square of a cemetery that had escaped his attention until now. He could not have chosen a more appropriate location for remorse, he thought. He had failed at life. What else was there than this place and all it implied?

At the low point of his damning self-assessment, his mind seemed to undergo a sudden, slight alteration, as subtle as the rising of a breeze. He felt more than actually heard a gentle prompting that seemed to come from either within his distracted imagination or somewhere in the funereal environment. It comforted him in a voiceless urging, a wordless persuasion, something to the effect that the coming eclipse would be very special, that it would entail a surprise gift beyond, yet part of, its obvious synchronicity with his birthday. How peculiar, to be thinking these thoughts, so at odds with his deep remorse! The feeling, almost a kind of heady euphoria, lingered a while longer, then seemed to evaporate, like a barely perceptible perfume wafted away on a breath of air. With it went his depression, and he found himself strangely indifferent to his catalogued failures. "What was that all about?" he wondered. Self-composed and intrigued by the experience, he descended the mountain with the evening sun.

"The eclipse has already started!" Juan, a local guide he'd engaged the day before, was banging on his hotel room door at 6:00 A.M. More asleep than awake, Vanderdecken threw on his clothes and grabbed a special pair of sunglasses. Juan was impatient but smiling a broad, toothy grin. He followed the American's fast walk through the narrow, still-dark corridor and down the stairs of the Hotel Las Lineas to his dilapidated 1961 Chevrolet parked on the street below. They sped out of town, going south from Nazca along the Panamerican Highway into the Peruvian desert. Every so often, they passed groups of people squinting up at the rising sun. He checked it out through the coal-black sunglasses he'd brought along for the event. Juan was right. The eclipse had already begun, although just barely.

Less than fifteen minutes out of Nazca, they were surrounded by an apparent infinity of gray desolation stretching from horizon to horizon. "There it is!" Vanderdecken had to yell over the blast of Juan's mufflerless engine, and Juan hauled the galloping jalopy off the highway, down a pitted gravel road toward the single, large rock outcropping standing black against an early morning sky. It was from this isolated prominence, selected a few days before, that the visiting American would view the eclipse. But the spot was not as solitary as he had anticipated. Even at this post-dawn hour there were about fifteen people gathered atop the twenty-foot high, three-hundred-foot long rock. He would not have the solitude he'd hoped for. "So be it," he thought.

By the time they found a place at the top, Vanderdecken could see, thanks to his special glasses, that the moon had only just begun to take its first bite out of the sun. The morning was mostly clear, with only a few clouds thinly veiling the east. Morning had already transformed the gray desert into golden brown, and the temperature of the dry air was increasing rapidly. Without appropriate shades, no one would have known there was anything unusual about today, at least at the beginning. But after the moon reached its halfway point across the sun, change began to accelerate. The swiftly rising heat of the desert reversed itself and dropped noticeably. The air got colder and colder, as the brightness of morning deepened into an Otherworldly shadow. By quickly advancing degrees, the golden desert hues turned silvery. Darkness at midmorning was falling upon this land of ancient empires. It intensified by perceptible increments, while an apparent unease swept among the small group of native people and foreign tourists. They spoke less often and in muted voices. The very rock on which they stood, watched, and waited turned black beneath their feet. "Maybe the sun won't come back, because we have been very bad," Juan muttered more to himself than to his companion, who looked at his face in the sinking twilight of the eastern morning sky. Juan was not smiling.

Then, so unexpectedly as to startle him, the mixed crowd of strangers began to yell and clap their hands for the sun's return. They made such a savage racket that their noise echoed far out over the desert. Their outburst struck him as historically ironic, because he recalled reading how both Native Americans and the Ancient Greeks, for all their high civilization, would scream for the moon to release the sun during a total eclipse. Here were human beings in 1994 A.D. continuing this tradition.

But things were to get still more dramatic. Just as the celestial conjunction reached its climax, casting its black cape over the face of the world, the eastern sky suddenly lit up with a hundred stars and weird constellations never seen before, except during the last total solar eclipse. Expressions of awe went up from the clapping observers. But almost as abruptly as they appeared, the unfamiliar stars faded into a steadily brightening heaven. The moon finally relinquished its grip on the sun, which restored light, heat, and color to the desert. Juan grinned self-consciously. "Well, maybe we weren't so bad after all!" His "superstitious" reaction to the eclipse seemed to mirror the unease exhibited by the crowd of observers.

The area chosen by Vanderdecken to view the phenomenon was among the Nazca lines. These are the famous, oversized drawings etched into the Pacific coastal desert two thousand and more years ago by artist-surveyors of a lost, little-understood civilization predating the Incas by centuries. Its geoglyphs are wonderful representations of a spider, monkey, whale, hummingbird, condor, trees, spirals, triangles, and lines that travel perfectly straight for miles over the desert. The earth-illustrations were executed on so colossal a scale that they may only be properly seen from the perspective of a circling airplane. Toward the southern end of this collection, bizarre as it is gigantic, sits the rock from which Vanderdecken witnessed his birthday eclipse. He knew nothing of the spot, save that it seemed the right place for observation. Later, on the night after the eclipse, he was reading a recently purchased book about the Nazca drawings. Turning to the middle of the book, he was surprised to see a photograph of the very rock he had used some fifteen hours before as the lookout for his early morning vigil.

A few sentences about the site described it as strangely unique, because it was the only place on the Nazca Plain from which exactly fifty absolutely straight lines radiate outward for miles in every direction. And it was from this very rock he saw the total solar eclipse that occurred on his fiftieth birthday. This was the "surprise gift" the mountain had whispered in promise to him the day before. He had not fantasized that wordless voice after all.

A tidal wave of powerful wonder swept over him, as he experienced a shuddering awe in that moment of recognition. He knew at once and with complete certainty that he had been guided by a providence as vast as time itself to commemorate his birth at this special place. It was as though the entire cosmos had celebrated his birthday. Standing on that rock, with its fifty coincidental lines etched into the desert thousands of years before, each one paralleling his own years of life, he had become the unwitting focal point of an incredibly unique moment, in which the sun, moon, and human prehistory perfectly aligned themselves through him. The deep, impenetrable mystery of the event galvanized his imagination. Its experience was beyond reason, almost beyond feeling. In the context of this experience, his feeling of a lifetime accumulation of insignificance was swept away forever.

Vanderdecken was filled instead with an overflowing sense of purpose and direction. He felt that his existence had meaning and value out of proportion to his previous self-assessment as a failure. The criteria he had used to arrive at such woefully inaccurate conclusions about himself had nothing whatsoever to do with the real aim of his destiny as a man singled out by nature herself to confirm his place in the grand scheme of the universe. It had done so because he needed such a miracle to save himself from despair. It was a miracle only he knew—naturally, because it was his birthday present from Creation.

He lapsed into a gentle, reassuring feeling, almost a settling of the soul. For the first time in his life, everything seemed in unerring harmony. The event had transformed him into a being of utter trust in the purposefulness of the universe. Henceforward, Vanderdecken walked through the world with serene confidence in himself and an ever-broadening compassion for all his fellow creatures, who, he knew, were no less interconnected to the same cosmic guidance that had directed his footsteps to that rock in the Peruvian desert under the total eclipse of a lifetime.

Both primitive and more advanced societies around the world have regarded eclipses of the sun with special dread. The very term comes from the Greek *ekleipsis*, or "failure," synonymous with "something gone drastically wrong." In a peculiar example of cultural comparisons, the Aztecs of Ancient Mexico likewise regarded each solar eclipse as a fundamental failure or aberration of the cosmos and consequently sacrificed aberrant human physical types (dwarves and hunchbacks) until the moon passed from the face of the sun. With the European Renaissance, such heavenly happenings were divested of their supernatural power to instill fear and generally understood in the cold, scientific light of celestial mechanics.

After Columbus arrived in the Americas, he used this understanding to coerce the indigenous people of Hispaniola into "volunteering" their services. Unwilling to perform further menial labor on behalf of their Spanish hosts, they laughed when he said he would take away the sun in the middle of the day unless they returned to work. Sure enough, after their refusal, Columbus raised his hand to the sky, which grew suddenly dark at his command. Panicked into subservience, the cowed natives vowed to resume their imposed duties, if only the admiral would bring back the sun. His pocket miracle had come by way of the Santa Maria's almanac, which listed all significant astronomical data and was standard issue aboard European ships of the time. Since then, people have regarded each solar eclipse as an infrequent curiosity, lovely and dramatic, to be sure, but nothing more. Even so, the same astronomers who reveal so much about this phenomenon provide us with additional clues to its enduring, underlying mystical significance.

In Earth skies, the sun looks no bigger than the moon. Their apparently equal size is an illusion caused by their vastly different distances from our planet. The moon's diameter is a mere 2,160 miles, roughly the distance from New York City to Phoenix, Arizona. The moon is about one-fourth the size of Earth, which it orbits at an average distance of 240,000 miles. The sun, in radical contrast, is an average 93 million miles away. Its diameter is 864,950 miles, 110 times the diameter of our world. In other words, if the sun were hollow, about four million of Earth's moons could fit inside it. Yet, these two vastly different spheres share a precisely exact size from our Earthbound perspective.

We all know how vital sunlight is to life, but evolutionary scientists only fairly recently discovered that our moon was an equal partner in creation. Their research tended to show that the first organic substances appeared in tidal pools caused by the lunar effect that still exerts its influence on our planet. It is to this so-called primordial soup of four billion years ago that all living things on Earth, humans included, trace their ultimate ancestry. The odds against the sun and moon, these two inconceivably different spheres, appearing as equals in our sky, seem so great as to be virtually unique in the universe. The odds grow greater still if we consider the chances of their paths intersecting as perfectly as they do several times per century, when moon and sun embrace in a total eclipse. We humans alone of Earth's creatures recognize this recurrent phenomenon. That fact in itself suggests each eclipse is significant, for not only purely astronomical but also spiritual reasons.

Our ancestors were afraid of an eclipse. They saw only the threatening, incongruent darkness, the apparent death, however temporary, of the life-giving sun. A more credible interpretation might have been to accept each eclipse as a spectacular covenant between humanity and the Infinite Mind. Brother Sun and Sister Moon gave us, and all Earth's creatures, birth. Yet, we must somehow be special, because only we appreciate the periodic conjunction of these two orbs, so unlike each other, but wonderfully similar in our unique sky. It seems impossible to believe that so perfect a match of such radically different celestial bodies is merely the result of blundering chance, especially when we consider the universal laws and illimitable organization that permeate the whole fabric of creation. Perhaps the eclipse was a final touch to that creation set in motion by the Creator, not to frighten mankind but to assure us that we have a high purpose and profound meaning in the vast scheme of things.

Seeing an eclipse as the precise opposite of any "failure," Vanderdecken, who experienced a transformational coincidence on his fiftieth birthday, believes that each solar eclipse is a sign of the faith the Creator has always had and will forever have in us: "He set it in the sky as a recurring reminder of our special covenant with Him and His work. As such, we should graciously accept the eclipse as a gift from heaven, the confirmation of our special destiny as a species."

Your Own Book of Fate

*The day of days, the great day of the feast of life, is that in
which the inward eye opens to the Unity of things. It is
not in us so much as we are in it.*

— Ralph Waldo Emerson, *Fate*

Beginning in 1993, I recorded in a diary every personal meaningful
coincidence, big and small, that happened to me. Four years of
logging these experiences showed they occurred on an average of
eight times per month—that is, about one hundred each year. The
vast majority, of course, tended to be forgotten.

But it was only in the agglomerate that they took on an unexpected momentousness. Viewed separately, they usually seemed
quaint or even fascinating, but their significance was not always
apparent. Seen in the broader context of other coincidences that
came before and after it, however, a single acausal event often
assumed tremendous relevance as the missing piece of a coherent
puzzle. Looking at a television an inch from the screen one will
see only dots, called pixels, many thousands of which make up the
televised image, which becomes comprehensible only from a

distance. So too, the greater image of our lives may be observed in its totality only when we see how each one of our meaningful coincidences joins together into a much larger, interrelated wholeness. Personal journals allow us to stand back and view all our synchronicities from a proper perspective. Their documentation affords us the objectivity necessary to appreciate the miraculous character of our existence. Recognizing this big picture is an awesome experience, very often life-changing, transformational in the highest sense, because, having recorded our own meaningful coincidences, we absolutely trust their credibility.

Like a high-flying reconnaissance aircraft mapping all the land features of a territory too enormous to be appreciated on the ground, we are able to trace unexpected, revealing patterns and cycles in our lives, including a sense of direction and guidance we may have never suspected. When we keep a synchronicity journal, the meanings and apparent intentions of each acausal event may become clear. In examining and deciphering such a paranormal chronicle we are, in effect, using a chart of our own unfolding destiny, in the same way the navigator of a ship uses the reliable map of an unknown region. The great benefit of recording meaningful coincidences is the certainty that overwhelms us, a deep, inner conviction that we are personally connected through our subconscious and everything in our surroundings to the Organizational Principle of the Universe, the Infinite Mind, the Creator—whatever one prefers to name the fountainhead of cosmic order.

Synchronicities are mostly little miracles through which an otherwise Unseen Consciousness manifests itself in our lives. They are the means by which that Consciousness communicates with us. We may speak to the gods in prayer, but significant coincidence is the medium whereby they speak to us.

Just as Earth's atmosphere is incessantly bombarded by particles from outer space that are all but invisible, save the less frequent, more dramatic shooting star, synchronicities are personal messages from the Otherworld that we constantly receive and generally ignore. Such phenomena do not occur capriciously or without reason. Rather, they are always, by the very nature of their definition, perfectly timed events to guide and direct us or pointedly comment on our condition. They therefore instill in anyone who recognizes them the conviction that our individual lives, however insignificant they may seem, are, in fact, highly significant, filled with purpose and laden with meaning. An appreciation of synchronicity as it applies to our own life must inevitably lead us to the most powerful sense of direction and an elevated objectivity, from which we view ourselves and our fellow creatures within the broader context of a fundamentally harmonious universe.

Synchronicity is our direct link with everyone's notion of God, from fundamentalist to physicist, from those who feel certain about their belief systems to others who honestly admit they question the existence of any divine personality. To understand our meaningful coincidences is to understand exactly who we are, our place in the grand scheme of existence, what we must do, where we are going and why.

These are problems humans continue to wrestle with after millennia of inconclusive debate. Yet, the answers have been around us all the time. No one can satisfy the basic questions of life for anyone else, because each person requires different answers. What is true for one individual may not necessarily be valid for anyone else. The life history and destiny of no two individuals are the same. Philosophers and theologians continue seeking general principles that may be applied to everyone, but their search has been in vain, because each one of us is as unique as our fingerprints. In view of our distinct identities, only we may determine what existence means for us. And since the universe is apparently trying to communicate with each individual through synchronicity, what we most need to know lies in the personal messages it sends us.

How to Organize and Use Your Synchronicity Journal

In order to read and understand your meaningful coincidences, you'll need some method to collect and preserve them. The most effective means for their documentation and deciphering is a journal. It will be a special book about yourself, co-authored with the Infinite Mind of Creation. After collecting your own meaningful coincidences for only a short time, you will realize that you have set up a dialogue with the Great Mystery itself, the Superconsciousness underlying the material universe and through which you are personally connected to it.

Since these communications from the Otherworld may be among the most valuable gifts you will ever receive, they must be documented in something befitting their importance. Jotting them down on scattered pieces of paper or on a looseleaf note pad cheapens them. Verbally reporting synchronous events into a tape recorder is not only similarly inappropriate; it's an awkward, less effective way to appreciate your synchronicities *in toto*. Over time, as your meaningful coincidences accumulate, tracing their growing number of associations and trying to view them as an interrelating whole will become increasingly unmanageable. You will be forced to readjust your overall perspective whenever your collected syn- chronicities grow more numerous, until simple objectivity collapses under the multiplicity of acausal events. Typing one's meaningful coincidences depersonalizes them, lessening their significance. Writing them down in pencil devalues them. Indeed, choosing the physical tools used to create your journal has as much to do with your subconscious as experiencing synchronicity itself.

Unless you already have the kind of utensils described here, your quest into meaningful coincidence should begin with new, unused instruments. The basic elements of your own journal of fate may be found at a good stationery store or bookstore. Choose two clothbound volumes different from each other but both with blank pages. A standard size that works well is 5 1/4 by 8 1/2 inches. Pick those that best reflect your personality. Keep in mind while making your selections that one of the books will be used to set down the acausal events you encounter, while in the other you will record your dreams. The latter volume is necessary not only to document instances of shared or synchronous dreams but for the exercise and development of your subconscious receptivity. In our research group we learned that individuals who maintained a dream diary concurrent with a synchronicity journal seemed to increase the frequency of meaningful coincidences and improve their perception. Keeping a record of your dreams makes it possible to trace recurring themes and patterns moving between the conscious and subconscious mind, often a surprising and revealing interpenetration that will enhance your appreciation of the synchronicity experience.

Select an ink pen that will be used only for recording in your journals. An old-fashioned fountain pen or a more modern cartridge pen is advisable, because it writes smoothly, but a ball-point pen will do, if it is of sufficient quality. Whatever your preference, make sure you are comfortable with it and that it is somehow special in its shape, color, or writing characteristics. You will also need another pen, one with a different color of ink, preferably red. These few tools, together with *Synchronicity & You*, are all you will need.

On the inside front page of the volume you choose for your synchronicity journal, vertically list the seventeen different categories of meaningful coincidence as identified in chapter 1: inanimate objects, numbers, environmental and animal ostenta, precognition, dreams (precognitive and shared), guidance, telepathy, parallel lives, origins, art, warnings, death, rescue, reincarnation, moira, enigmas, and transformational experiences. Number them sequentially from 1 to 17.

With the black- or blue-colored ink pen, succinctly describe your most recent meaningful coincidence. Write it down straightforwardly, as you would a report, mentioning as many details as possible, including the people involved, locations, and your state of mind at the time. Avoid any kind of judgment or interpretation. Do not endeavor to connect the event with anything outside itself, either other coincidences or dreams. Try to isolate the synchronicity within the limited scope of its own occurrence. Above all, be clear and accurate in your description. Take as much space as you feel is necessary to complete the report. Whether it is set down in a few sentences or developed over the course of several pages is unimportant; the important thing is that the coincidence be recorded in clear language. When recording any meaningful coincidence, always include the date it took place in its own space just above the entry. If possible, add the hour and minute it occurred next to the date.

After you have made the entry, go to the categories you listed on the inside cover. Select the classification that best fits your coincidence and, with the red- or other-colored ink pen, write its number just in front of the date.

Now go to the bottom of the entry. Skip a line or space, then describe your reaction and interpretation using the same red- or other-colored pen. Again, write as little or as much as you believe is needed to cover all your thoughts on the occurrence. Mark the date nearby. Leave the next page blank. You may come back to this empty page sometime in the future, after you find that the coincidence you reported is connected to others or to something else in your life, such as dreams or complementary events. Always use the red- or other-colored ink pen to write all commentary.

Entries in the companion dream journal are similarly dated and described with the black- or blue-ink pen, with commentary in red beneath. Many people have difficulty remembering their dreams. They should be recorded as soon as possible after waking, because they become increasingly difficult to remember with the passage of even a few minutes. It is not uncommon to go days, weeks, or even longer without sufficient recall of a single dream. But describing those we are able to remember can sometimes play pivotal roles in the synchronous events we seek to chronicle and decipher.

While most dreams do not appear to have any bearing on synchronicity, it is important to faithfully record them for the rare instance when one of them interfaces with our waking existence. These are moments of wonderful numinosity and invariably of deep significance for anyone who experiences them. Beyond the infrequent dream that leafs over from the sleep state into our conscious lives, paying attention to our dreams, accepting them as personal communications from the Otherworld of our subconscious, improves our awareness of the mystical element that lives in and around us. We thereby become more sensitive to the synchronous character of our world and develop skills for subtle observation and appreciation of life's magical drama, in which we play a role.

Both the synchronicity journal and the dream diary will take on greater significance with time. The more their pages fill with reports of meaningful coincidences, the more we feel the presence of the miraculous in our lives. It is essential to record every synchronicity, no matter how trivial, ridiculous, or pointless it may seem at first. Often a coincidence that does not appear worth noticing at first develops later into a connecting element of decisive significance. If we wait to set down only those events that are obvious for their miraculous qualities, our journal will not do us much good. It is only in the aggregate that we may grasp the full scope of synchronicity in our lives, when every known instance of this phenomenon is preserved for us to fit into a broader context. Like the individual stone of a mosaic, each piece is meaningless, until, from a proper perspective, we can see its deliberate arrangement with many others to form a whole artwork.

When just beginning synchronicity journals, some individuals can be easily disappointed, because meaningful coincidences are not immediately forthcoming. If you have not paid much attention to such events before, you might be expecting too much. The appearance of acausality usually begins slowly, almost hesitantly, for individuals new to it, but it gradually accelerates with time and will eventually manifest itself in almost a bombardment of occurrences. Moreover, just as with falling in love (which is itself a kind of synchronicity), you are less likely to find a meaningful coincidence if you look for it instead of allowing it to happen and being prepared to acknowledge it when it finally appears. In the realm of synchronicity, you are not in control. You permit a higher control to enter your life.

You neither surrender to it nor try to dominate it, but instead cooperate with it. Your only measure of control is your decision to follow the messages embodied in the meaningful coincidences sent to you or to ignore them. There is no punishment, no blame or guilt, no standardized conception of right or wrong at stake. Synchronicity is ours to do with as we please.

Decoding Synchronicity

To scrutinize something like synchronicity is to diminish it. We murder when we dissect. In trying to understand this phenomenon, the degree to which we analyze it determines how it either divulges itself or escapes us. Indeed, it is less important that we consciously understand a meaningful coincidence than that we allow ourselves to feel it. What we may never understand intellectually we more certainly grasp subconsciously, with other ways of knowing.

People long in contact with synchronous events believe humans have more ways of knowing than most of us realize. They regard the rational mind as a jealous tyrant who, afraid of losing control, needs to dominate all things at all times and refuses to recognize our intuitive capacity for knowledge through feeling. A concertgoer who confines his attention to the scientific principles of air set in motion through certain vibrations generated by wooden and metal instruments will hear various frequencies of sound, but no music.

What, then, are we to do with all these synchronicities we collect? Let us unravel them gently, as we would any particularly precious gift we receive. If we tear into them, they are sure to get damaged. They may even stop coming altogether. Certainly, the first, best, and most effective means by which to access any meaningful coincidence is to immerse oneself in the awe of it. Opening ourselves to feel the thrill of its magic allows it to trip any number of subconscious switches that turn on our inner enlightenment. Freely bathing our spirit in the peculiar sensation induced by a synchronous event sets all our nonrational ways of knowing in action. Rather than passing off such incidents as transient curiosities to be dismissed, inevitable probabilities, or incidents of no importance, by honoring and acknowledging them we step up their power to move and inform us. Only from this inspirational basis can we make any conventionally logical interpretations.

After we have opened ourselves to its emotional impression, we may attempt to access the coincidence by consulting our categories for the best fit. In the previous chapter, we read how Philip Vanderdecken relished the powerful synchronicities he encountered in Peru. Had he allowed his rationalizing pessimism to discount the meaningful coincidences that presented themselves to him, he would have deprived them of their significance. Instead, he gave free vent to his natural capacity for wonder. He sought less to intellectualize his mystical experiences than to develop an appreciation for them by savoring their magic. This capacity or willingness to *allow* synchronicity is the best general method for opening ourselves to understanding the phenomenon. Complex rituals and profound meditation may prepare certain initiates for the onset of mystical phenomena of all kinds. But such complicated methods are not as effective or necessary as the proper receptivity we achieve through simply allowing ourselves the possibility of experiencing meaningful coincidences.

Their descriptions should shed at least some light on the happening. Rationalizing such events will dissolve their significance. Only if we examine them in the light of our initial emotional response to their arrival may we come to a correct understanding of what they mean. At first, their meaning may utterly elude us. Only later, after we have traced their connections to other, related, occurrences, will they reveal themselves. The fundamental principle in the interpretation of any synchronicity is this: The person to whom it is directed is best qualified to comprehend it and should be the final judge of its significance. We must not allow ourselves to be persuaded by any outside influence. The relationship between a meaningful coincidence and its recipient is intimate, and final decisions on what it is trying to convey rest entirely with the person involved.

Other than allowing yourself to experience the dramatic force of synchronicity and respecting your own feelings above all others in its interpretation, a particularly effective approach to accessing any meaningful coincidence is meditation. Many people have wildly inaccurate notions about meditation, imagining it is some kind of pretentious flimflam foisted by phony gurus on their gullible followers. For our purposes, meditation is nothing more than a clearing out of all the mental dross that piles up inside the conscious mind. Meditation is a psychological cleaning technique to empty our thought processes of the inessential, while opening them up for new insights. Meditation is particularly useful for getting rid of distractions, while improving one's powers of concentration. Problems come into clearer focus as we emotionally center around some inner still-point. In such a clear frame of mind, the meaning of a synchronous occurrence that stubbornly refuses to yield itself to direct assaults of logic may suddenly reveal itself.

The simplest of these subtler strategies is ordinary sleep. Just as you feel yourself drifting into unconsciousness, review the coincidence in your mind without any attempt to understand it, but with the desire to know its meaning. If a solution is not forthcoming, repeat the process on several additional nights. The mind at rest allows for the recycling and sometimes the reprocessing of problems that concern our consciousness. You can expect three possible outcomes to your nightly inquiry. An answer could be on your lips in the morning; it could manifest itself in the psychodrama of sleep (another good reason to keep a dream journal!); or it might connect with another coincidence, which will probably elucidate the original problem to some degree but might also compound its mystery.

There are many methods available. For a valuable introduction to the subject, I recommend Naomi Humphrey's *Meditation: The Inner Way*. A simple procedure that works along with the best of them lasts only thirty to forty minutes and involves nothing more complicated than counting your breaths. First, find a time, place, and space where you will not be disturbed. Shut the door, unplug the telephone, and do whatever else is necessary to ensure your complete privacy for just half an hour to forty minutes. Sit on the floor, in a chair, in any position you feel most comfortable—but do not lie down, because you want to avoid sleep. Meditation must be a conscious activity that leads to subconscious insight.

Close your eyes, take a deep breath through your nostrils. Breathe in as deeply as you can, all the while imagining that you are breathing in clarity and goodness. Hold your breath for seven counts, then breathe slowly out your mouth, between your lips, as though gently blowing out a candle. As you do so, imagine you are breathing out all distractions, worries, concerns, depression, and anything else negative. Repeat the deep breathing twice more. Now breathe normally, your eyes still shut. Count the exhale of every breath from one to seven, from seven to one; from one to fourteen, then back down to one; then from one to twenty-one and back down again to one—thus by sevens to the count of forty-two and back to one.

Think only of the number of breaths you are counting, nothing else. Especially for beginners, both external sounds and internal thoughts are distracting. Unless so demanding they require immediate attention, they will not ruin the meditation. At the approach of any distraction, do not fight it or try to banish it from your thoughts. Instead, think something like, "This short space of time is my own. I will have the rest of the day to deal with all my ordinary problems. Now I will get on with counting my breaths." You may even lose your place in the count. This does not matter at all; just begin again where who imagine you might have left off.

After counting back down to one from forty-two, quietly consider the coincidence you have not been able to understand. Do not try to decode it now, either. Simply go over it in your mind, examining it from various points of view as you would a lovely vase, less in any attempt to learn something particular about it than simply to appreciate its beauty. Finally, express your desire to someday know what the occurrence signifies. If you indeed come to decipher its meaning, well and good. If not, you will continue to graciously accept synchronicity for the gift it is and welcome its mysterious contribution to your destiny. Take three long breaths in the same manner in which you began the meditation.

Meditation is the most effective technique available to us in prompting coincidences to give up their meanings. But we must not be impatient and expect instant results. Answers have been known to manifest themselves soon after and even during meditation, but such appearances are not common. More likely, if you continue to maintain something like the proper kind of centered receptivity acquired during your meditative session, answers will come in any variety of settings. Additional meditation, at your leisure and convenience, may succeed where a single sitting did not. In fact, meditation should not be used solely for trying to decipher meaningful coincidences. Regular use, regardless of any specific intentions, substantially enhances our sensitivity to grasp more readily and deeply so much in our surroundings. It also allows our subconscious greater access to our waking hours and even seems, according to some individuals, to increase the frequency and range of acausality itself.

Renowned physicists Wilbur, Russell, Combs, and Holland, who have written extensively on meaningful coincidences, believe their frequency increases with meditation. It blurs sharp distinctions between the conscious and subconscious mind, thereby freeing the images of universal archetypes, "which in turn lie at the root of synchronicity" (Grasse, p. 39). Ray Grasse agrees that meditation cultivates "a spirit of receptivity" for acausal events of personal significance (p. 84).

Seven Steps to Understanding Your Own Book of Fate

The proper method for understanding synchronicity and its role in our lives is sevenfold:

1. Acknowledge meaningful coincidence as an important message directed to you personally by the Infinite Mind of the Universe (or whatever name you prefer for the organizing principle behind all material existence).
2. Allow yourself to feel the mystical power of your experience.
3. Record meaningful coincidences in your journal.
4. Try to identify each personal synchronous event with one of the seventeen specified categories.
5. Trust your feelings and your own judgment above all other sources of information.
6. Use meditation to access the meaning of each synchronicity.
7. Give yourself time to make sense of the meaningful coincidences in your life. Try to see each coincidence within the context of your growing collection of such events. Be patient. Be grateful if answers come. Be accepting if they do not.

The sense of wonder in your own life will expand as you keep your synchronicity journal. You can fill its pages with a growing number of personal miracles that will continue to astonish you for years to come. They will give you an ever-deepening feeling of purpose, direction, and self-worth more convincing than anything else in your experience. You will feel intimately connected to the organizing will of the entire universe. You will know that you are an integral part of its destiny. Limitless potential for self-mastery, genuine inner peace, and compassion for and harmony with all your fellow creatures lies in your developing understanding of meaningful coincidence. The enlightenment sought for so long by so many via so many paths that only dead-ended in disillusionment has always been within our immediate grasp. Its attainment is simple and direct. You do not need any guru to lead you to his or her notion of meaning, nor must you forsake the world for a lifetime of self-imposed abnegation as a monk. You are not required to spend hours at a time in prayer. The answer need not be learned at any long, expensive seminar given by a self-declared expert, nor in any books or magazines, save your own book of fate.

The empty stare of blank pages from your new synchronicity journal may seem somewhat intimidating at first. What are you supposed to do? Wait around for the next meaningful coincidence? The very nature of the phenomenon as a surprising, atypical incident means its occurrences are irregular and unexpected. Almost certainly, if you deliberately look for such an event, you will not find it. Allowing synchronicity to happen is not the same as expecting it. Cultivate instead an awareness of the nuances in your existence, a kind of detached observation, and the acausal will appear in its own good time.

There are, however, several methods to encourage meaningful coincidences. Expecting them in certain anticipation tends to put off their appearance, but maintaining a level of awareness for the subtleties of life is necessary in order to recognize and appreciate synchronicity when it occurs. We should strive for a mental balance between anticipation and awareness. Meditation not only improves our sensitivities and powers of recognition, but may itself lead to meaningful coincidences, perhaps because this mental discipline is such a proven method of establishing harmony with the rhythms of life.

Traveling unquestionably encourages synchronous experiences, because in traveling we are moving through the field of time and its direct interaction with our material world. The pursuit of our *moira*, whatever it is that gives us extraordinary feelings of fulfillment, generates perhaps the highest frequency and most insightful intensity of meaningful coincidences. It is as though we were being confirmed and encouraged by some higher, unseen, but deeply personalized consciousness to "follow our bliss."

Certainly, the most effective method for bringing about synchronicity in your life is to be passionately engaged in that which most interests you. Collecting stamps or white-water rafting, silently appreciating a flower garden or skydiving from an airplane—whatever especially appeals to the deepest, most genuine level of your identity is your source for personal synchronicity. Appealing to the thing that validates your life, something you recognize as particularly authentic (although it may not be authentic for anyone else), is the surest way to generate meaningful coincidences.

Synchronous events constellate especially around intense personal involvement, particularly involvement in inspiring, uplifting, or enlightening activities. A simple way to spark synchronicity is to be so engrossed in reading a book that it pulls your imagination into the author's world. A member of our research group, Henry O'Connell, once found a biography of Judy Garland, somebody he was interested in for a few years but had never had the opportunity to learn about until he stumbled on this biography. Not far into its first chapter, he began to notice the first acausal events connecting him to Judy Garland. O'Connell would randomly turn on his radio to hear some old recording she'd made fifty years before; sometimes she would be singing the very song just described in her biography. Friends unaware of the book he was so profoundly engaged in would unexpectedly bring up the same stage in her career he'd just finished reading about. Quite unintentionally, he kept coming across photographs of her. One day, he was musing on this series of coincidences, when he found himself, by sheer accident, at a downtown skyscraper known as the Garland Building. Synchronicities came thicker and faster as O'Connell immersed himself more deeply in the story of Judy Garland.

Love relationships are common breeding grounds for meaningful coincidences. Traveling, as mentioned previously, also stimulates their appearance. But by far the most effective means for conjuring synchronicity is to be passionately involved in the pursuit of your deepest desire. It is as though the Universal Mind itself were cheering on one's dedication to living the authentic life. Whether it is model railroading or writing the Great American Novel, gardening or finding the cure for cancer, all that matters is that one's heart be engaged. To be passionately involved with anything or anyone is to attract the energies of creation in the form of meaningful coincidence. To be true to your innermost being by acting on its behalf and actually following through on your highest desires will set up a sympathetic resonance with the underlying vibrational frequencies of nature. They will respond to your activated heartstrings in the same manner in which the strings of a violin, set aside and untouched, will begin vibrating to the vibrations of another violin being played nearby.

The key, then, to attracting synchronicity into your life is to find your own passion, whatever it may be, and awaken it. Whether or not this awakening is in any manner considered successful or unsuccessful in the eyes of others or in the opinion of the whole world is of absolutely no consequence. The greatest poetry written today is not being published. Many of the noblest acts of human compassion and self-sacrifice are either neglected or vilified. Yet, anyone who strives to live, even occasionally, in accord with his or her ultimate truth will find confirmation and even blessing from the Great Mystery through glittering showers of synchronicity—cosmic awards for individual heroism personally presented by the Master Builder of the Universe, because you are sharing in the same work.

chapter 10

Synchronicity, Key to the Ultimate Mystery

*This relation between the mind and matter is not fancied
by some poet, but stands in the will of God, and so is free
to be known to all men. The universe becomes transparent, and the light of higher laws than its own shines
through it.*

—Ralph Waldo Emerson, *Nature*

In the preceding pages, we have pinned down several definitions of synchronicity, boxed it in seventeen categories, and harnessed its power in a journal. But have we come any closer to really understanding how and why it works?

Perhaps some answers may be found by observing the synchronous experience itself. As mentioned near the close of the last chapter, the rate at which meaningful coincidences occur appears to increase with meditation. The implication here is that synchronicity operates at a subconscious level. Our conscious mind, which plays no role in the coincidence itself, is useful only for recognizing the connection while it is taking place or shortly thereafter. At best, reason may strive to interpret its significance, to discover its "meaning," but our capacities for logic in such matters are feeble gropings compared to the immediacy and totality of intuitive insight. By softening the distinction otherwise so clearly drawn between wakefulness and unconsciousness, meditation allows our innate receptivity to operate more openly and with less opposition from our mental control center.

The meditative state approaches the subconscious state, that darker recess wherein lie potentialities unacknowledged, suppressed, and feared by the rationally dominating mind. As David Peat writes, "Synchronicities represent a bridge between matter and mind" (Peat, p. 5).

Instances of synchronicity are also multiplied by travel and increased social interaction. Beyond the obvious increased opportunities it provides for encountering meaningful coincidences, travel is itself a transformational experience. Our state of consciousness is altered when we physically move from one environment into new surroundings. Travel is transition, physically and emotionally. The same sense of transition takes place in relationships.

Still, the surest method for conjuring synchronous events into one's life is to be passionately involved in something, especially if it is greater than oneself. Whether intensely researching an interesting term paper or fervently at work in a flower garden, wherever one's heart is most engaged, there also are to be found the most coincidences. Anyone deeply committed to some absorbing activity knows that time speeds up whenever they are so engaged. To the artist thoroughly immersed in his work from nine in the morning until five in the afternoon, his hours seemed to shrink into minutes. Hours, minutes, seconds, and even days do not pass this way for others not so engaged. It is as though this acceleration of time creates a transdimensional vortex in which standard perceptions of reality are deformed, just as light rays in outer space are bent by the vortex of a black hole. Passion, however expressed, is itself an altered state of consciousness, which opens our interior potentials, normally caged by the rational mind. When asked by a newspaper reporter to explain his theory of relativity for the public, Albert Einstein replied that one minute a man spends kissing his girlfriend will pass much faster than if he had to spend the same length of time sitting atop a hot stove.

To exemplify passionate involvement as the subconscious mainspring for psychic activity, Jung cited the results of J. B. Rhine's controlled studies on extrasensory perception (ESP). A consistent factor in his tests was a perfect correlation between the success of a subject in correctly answering ESP-related questions and his or her enthusiasm for the project. A decline in attentiveness was paralleled by a falling off of correct responses. If the same subject's emotional involvement could be stimulated, his or her test scores improved to levels commensurate with the subject's interest.

The human capacity for deep involvement seems to act like a dynamic attracter that sets up an energy field just as invisible and powerful as the static electricity produced by a mechanical generator. The reason may lie in the natural affinity of like for like. Perhaps the very energy given off by the creative process itself, whether in the storm that generates lightning or the human storm of productive action, is one and the same power. If this is true, then we may begin to understand the real origins of synchronicity.

Meaningful coincidences do not, as many psychologists affirm, lie entirely within the subconscious mind, because they require something outside the individual intellect with which to connect. Arguments that acausal events occur when some subconscious need interprets or even affects the exterior environment may explain some instances of synchronicity, but they certainly do not explain all or even the majority. According to Combs and Holland, "the investigators who followed Jung all tended to approach syn-chronicity from one direction only, from the world of experience, dreams, fantasies, and the unconscious" (Grant, p. 226). But even Combs and Holland, although they expanded the discussion by examining it from the standpoint of new and relevant discoveries in modern physics, simultaneously delimited it, however much those limits might have been pushed back, because a nonmaterial phe-nomenon must forever elude the material criteria used to nail it down. Using physics to capture the meaning of synchronicity is like trying to photograph a dream.

Parapsychologists point to synchronicity to validate the reality of telepathy, reincarnation, and all the rest of their favorite anomalies. But meaningful coincidence only sometimes uses para-normal episodes as vehicles to manifest itself. Parapsychology may occasionally be the means, but it is never the end of significant acausality. Theologians oversimplify synchronicity by claiming it is just the will of Heaven, which, although perhaps very fundamentally correct in a general cosmic sense, explains nothing and misleads inquirers into interminable digressions about the identity of God. Most philosophers go to the opposite extreme, obscuring the phenomenon with a welter of obtuse theories far beyond any helpful consensus. For all their occasional flashes of disparate insight, they never shine enough credible light into the nuts and bolts of synchronicity.

For all our vaunted modern technology, the ancients appear to have had a far better grasp of synchronicity than almost anyone since. Of course, the term is a modern one, invented by Jung, but people have recognized synchronicity long before him, though they gave it different names such as ostenta, moira, and destiny. As I hope I have demonstrated in the preceding chapters, theology, philosophy, physics, psychology, and even parapsychology are inadequate to explain it. The modern scientific attitude has become so specialized that no one is taken seriously outside their proscribed field of expertise, and scientists seem more interested in trashing each other's theories and jealously guarding their specialized departments than they are in developing a bigger picture of existence. Yet, these disciplines are the only means used to investigate acausality. What we do not have that the ancients had is a willingness to make unprejudiced conclusions based on the evidence of direct experience.

The classical Greeks based all their science on their powers of keen observation and persistent openmindedness. Out of this broader approach arose the birth of true scientific thought. And it is still the only method whereby the mystery of meaningful coincidence may be accessed. If we see that, because of this unrestricted, wider view, the Greeks and other peoples of former times did indeed have a clearer comprehension of meaningful coincidence, we might begin to understand just how it continues to operate for us. Because synchronicity is an eternal, timely, yet timeless marvel, we have no cause to imagine that it functioned any differently thousands of years ago than it does today, just as other aspects of nature operate in the same manner now as then. Unfortunately, most of the wisdom of the ancient world was lost with the fall of classical civilization. Even before that unmatched human catastrophe, esoteric ideas were largely secreted within the closed societies of mystery cults, religions, schools, and brotherhoods. But enough fragmented material still survives to provide subsequent generations with at least a glimpse of past knowledge.

Heraclitus, a Greek philosopher in the fourth century B.C., wrote of a Logos, or cosmic "reason," through which all things are interrelated and all natural events take place. He saw the universe as a coherent system in which changes were not isolated happenings but had repercussions across the entire fabric of existence. Change in one direction must, he believed, cause change in another direction, because all things were linked by an unseen connection, a web of organization deliberately created by the Logos. In his acceptance of the formal unity of the world of experience, Heraclitus argued that it was humankind's task to discover and understand the principles that bound all living and inorganic things together in an overall common purpose.

In his assertion that energy and matter are essentially indistinguishable from each other, he anticipated the same conclusion made by quantum physicists 2,500 years later. Modern science now knows that at the atomic particle level, matter and energy interchange and space and time fuse into a continuum. Interaction takes place even between the observer and the observed. It is from this "elemental fire," or energy, Heraclitus said that everything is born. But it is ruled over by Aion, a boy, the Divine Child, the Sacred Androgyne, combining within himself the blended elements of a male-female duality that permeates creation. He is the personification of time in its capricious, unpredictable aspect, because Aion, this ultimate ruler of existence, was portrayed gambling eternally on a game board, a metaphor for meaningful coincidence. Resorting to the same analogy Heraclitus used twenty-four centuries before, Ralph Waldo Emerson characterized an interrelationship between the universal realm of nature and human thought as "two boys pushing each other on the curbstone of the pavement" (Emerson, p. 276).

Hippocrates, born about twenty years after the death of Heraclitus, pursued a similar line of thought: "There is one common flow, a common breathing. Everything is in sympathy. The whole organism and each one of its parts are working together for the same purpose. The great principle extends to the most extreme part, and from the extremest part returns again to the great principle" (Grant, p. 137).

These early Greek ideas about the universe's temporal dimension reached their final expression in Plato's 4th century B.C. definition of time as the moving image of eternity (*The Timaeus*).

Philo of Alexandria, a contemporary of Jesus, perpetuated Heraclitus's concept of the Logos as an intermediary between God and humans, which is as good as admitting that meaningful coincidences are the means by which the Creator communicates with his creatures. His belief that individual providence can suspend the perceived laws of nature is an early definition of synchronicity. The self-evidence of these acts of providence established God's existence, he argued, although they did not reveal the enigma of His essence or identity. Philo's originality in espousing these ideas has since been called into question, since they appear to have been some of the leading concepts circulating among the mystery schools of his time and long before. His debt to Heraclitus, as just mentioned, was obvious enough, and Philo's use of such esoteric terms as *enthousiasmos* clearly shows he was at least strongly influenced by the mystery schools (Grant, p. 507).

Enthousiamos means "having God within oneself." It refers to the proposition that God is not some bearded, anthropomorphic autocrat personally wielding omnipotence and enthroned in the clouds, entirely above and outside of His own creation. Instead, He is the unifying spirit of existence that dwells within everyone and everything and is, consequently, the common, invisible thread tying each fragment of the universe together. In short, He is not only *out there*, but likewise *in here*. This term certainly helps define synchronicity, which operates on the principle of meaningful connections established by some unseen force between our inner being and our outer experience.

Two centuries later, such ideas were still being developed by the Roman thinker Agrippa, who spoke of a World Soul "that penetrates all things. The soul of the world therefore is a thing in itself. It fills and bestows all things, binding and knitting together everything." Existence was not dominated by the four elements (earth, wind, fire, and water), he believed, "but by a certain fifth thing, having its being above and beside them." Agrippa's contemporary,

Plotinus, was the most influential philosopher of late antiquity. In the Enneads he wrote, "Chance has no place in life, but only harmony and order reign therein" (Grant, p. 515).

Nor were these unifying concepts confined to the ancient civilizations of the West. The Hindu religious poem Bhagavadgīta uses specific terminology to define the synchronous elements of creation. Brahman, for example, is the fundamental connection of all things in the universe, together with the energy and events that interact among them. The appearance of this universal oneness in the human soul is known as Atman. An indication of the deep antiquity of these seemingly advanced concepts is shown in Atmen, the word for "breath" in German, whose Indo-European roots go back to ancestral beginnings on the Steppes of Central Russia, five thousand and more years ago. Zen Buddhism uses the word *satori* to define the sense of unity one feels with the universe and a simultaneous awareness of the compassionate intelligence that permeates its every detail.

The doctrine of *pratitya-samutpada*, the "origination by dependence" or "the mutual arising," is regarded by millions of Buddhists in Tibet, China, and Korea as the motive principle of the universe and the interplay of occurrences through the unavoidable influences that all living beings exert on themselves and all matter. Pratitya-samutpada is the woven flux of phenomenal events occurring in series, one interrelating set generating the next, in which matter connects with the human psyche. In Japan, *kegon* ("garland" or "wreath") refers to the harmonious totality of existence, in which all the elements of creation are interdependent and interrelated, permeating everything. All living things, actions, and materials are strung together into a kind of invisible garland or string of pearls, each reflecting all the others.

Chi is the ancient Chinese "life force" still used in geomancy, the fitting of human dwellings within the spiritual contours of the natural environment. The very symbol of China, the dragon, represents this unseen power that energizes all things. The back of the dragon resembles and signifies China's mountains, which are alive with chi, being accumulations and focal points of the genius loci, the "spirit of place."

Across the sea, in ancient Mexico, the Mayas developed the concept of *chu-lel*, their word for the underside of nature, which they believed was unified in harmonious action by a universally governing intelligence. Proof of its existence was found in the observable balance of nature, from the regular rotation of the seasons and all their attendant plant and animal interactivity to the regular rotation of the heavens above. Everything the Mayas saw evidenced the synchronized cooperation of function and motion among living and nonliving matter.

Among all the Indian tribes north of the Rio Grande, the vision quest forms the single most important undertaking individuals experience in their lifetime. It involves a purification and self-denial undertaken to achieve an altered state of consciousness in which one can perceive signs or visitations in the form of guidance from another dimension. As the Native American shaman Medicine Grizzly Bear Lake explains, "there are indeed two separate but interrelated worlds of existence, the physical and the spiritual" (Lake, p. 27). Each vision quest is itself a transformational event, in that the person undergoing its rigors is a youngster on the verge of adolescence. The psychophysical changes he or she is experiencing are to be reflected in the meaningful changes of nature, into which the quester has been immersed with the proper receptivity induced through fasting and ritual conditioning. They may then be open to the kinds of ostenta, both natural and animal, described in chapter 2. The signs, portents, or messages they receive (almost invariably in the form of universal archetypes) are embraced as life-changing and remembered and nurtured unto death. The Osage, a subgroup of Siouan linguistic stock originally from the Atlantic Coast, maintain their deeply ancient concept of Wakonda, "the mysterious power," which infuses all humankind with the rhythms of nature and destiny. It is also known as Eawawonaka, or "the cause of our being."

After the fall of classical civilization, some European scholars dusted off the subject of synchronicity and once again took up its investigation. Foremost among these was Gottfried Wilhelm Leibniz, the seventeenth-century philosopher and mathematician whose direct influences on Western thought are still at work today. Only a very few examples of his long-lasting effect on the world include the theoretical ancestor of the modern computer and his work in such modern fields of research as submarines, the creation of scientific geology, and the desalinization of seawater. In *On the Art of Combination* (*De Arte Combinatoria*), he promoted the idea of a preestablished harmony in nature, in which there was an absolute synchronism of physical and psychic events. Foreshadowing Jung and Campbell, Leibniz held that the world was a well-regulated dream in which the same basic set of images belonged to all human beings. The metaphysical system he sought to perfect was based on a universal cause for all being (Krassner, p. 49).

The thought patterns Leibniz set in motion rippled into the nineteenth century, when even a novelist like Anatole France, who had once bitterly satirized the occult, could observe, "Chance is the pseudonym God uses when He does not want to sign His name" (Bach, p. 15). But it was Arthur Schopenhauer who confronted the problem of meaningful coincidence for the first time since the demise of classical civilization. His "Transcendent Speculation on the Apparent Deliberateness in the Fate of the Individual" "originally stood godfather," in Jung's own words, to Jung's concept of synchronicity. The Swiss psychologist took his start from lines such as these: "That occult power that guides even external influences can ultimately have its root only in our own mysterious inner being; for indeed in the last resort the alpha and omega of all existence lie within us" (Schopenhauer, p. 312).

But in his primal essay, Schopenhauer was not advocating any particular solution of synchronous events; he was examining the mystery from various points of view, of which the psychological was but one. His uncertainty is exemplified in this excerpt: "There is generally to be found everywhere a *mundus intelligibilis* that rules over chance itself....But what we here assume as operative is not nature, but the metaphysical that lies beyond nature and exists whole and undivided in every individual to whom, therefore, all this is of importance. To get to the bottom of these things, we should indeed first have to answer the following questions: is a complete disparity possible between a man's character and fate? or, looking at the main point, does the fate of everyone conform to his character? or finally, does a secret inconceivable necessity, comparable to the author of a drama, actually fit the two together always suitably?" (Schopenhauer, p. 312). Echoing Leibniz and anticipating Jung, Schopenhauer nonetheless hearkened back much earlier to the ancients' belief in a Universal Mind, when he concluded, "The subject of the great dream of life is in a certain sense only one thing, the will-to-live, and that all plurality of phenomena is conditioned by time and space. It is the great dream that is dreamed by that one entity, but in such a way that all its persons dream it together. Thus all things encroach on and are adapted to one another" (Schopenhauer, p. 307).

The only modern thinker to synthesize ancient belief in a universal intelligence underlying nature with present-day science was the French paleontologist Pierre Teilhard de Chardin. Ordained a Catholic priest in 1911, he won the Legion of Honour during World War I for his courage on the frontlines as a stretcher bearer, was a highly respected teacher at the Catholic Institute of Paris, and later traveled to China, where he played a major role in the discovery of Peking Man's skull, a find that pushed back human evolution by another quarter-million years. His subsequent research of Asian fossil deposits altered the development of twentieth-century paleontology.

Despite these influential achievements, Teilhard de Chardin's ideas about evolution and its spiritual implications were suppressed during his lifetime by his religious superiors, who likewise prevented him from teaching at the College de France. All his metaphysical work had to be published posthumously.

Teilhard de Chardin's deepening understanding of human evolution combined with his undiminished spiritual feelings to convince him that the invisible underside of the world's biosphere was an ordering intelligence—a noosphere, or "mental sphere," into which every human mind was subconsciously tuned. Influences, he said, were reciprocal, with the combined mental activity of humankind morphing the whole world, just as the noosphere organized humankind and the rest of nature. Individuals experience this interconnectedness when they feel their moods influenced by the emotional state of another human being or even their pets. Teilhard de Chardin's concept was foreshadowed in the previous century by Emerson, who speculated about "ideas in the air" generated by humankind's collective consciousness: "We are all impressionable, for we are made of them; all impressionable, but some more than others, and these first express them" (Emerson, p. 666).

Teilhard de Chardin went further to coin the term *cosmogenesis*, according to which the purpose of the noosphere was to make humankind the goal of all its striving, because human beings alone of all creatures on Earth are able to recognize the Universal Mind, consciously interact with it, and thereby transcend it (Chardin, p. 44). In this, he was echoing Friedrich Nietzsche, who regarded humans as "something to be surpassed;" this similarity alarmed Church authorities.

Teilhard de Chardin's likening of his noosphere to an invisible web binding up existence hearkens back to the deeply ancient *Rig Veda*, with its song of the great net of spiritual causality cast over the world by Indra. Scholars who have been led to elaborate on essentially the same conclusion, whether or not they knew anything about the Rig Veda, have often used the metaphor of a web or net to describe the binding together of all matter, energy, and action. "All those causal chains," Schopenhauer wrote, "that move in the direction of time, now form a large, common, much-interwoven net which with its whole breadth likewise moves forward in the direction of time and constitutes the course of the world" (Schopenhauer, p. 305). Japanese Buddhists who recognize the principle of kegon believe all matter and phenomena are attached to the strands of a cosmic web, at the center of which is located the Buddha, from whom spiritual power radiates throughout the universe. Their imagery recurs in the modern thought of writer Gwen Frostic: "We must bring about a total interplay of all our senses, develop a deep reverence for life that will not let us crush a growing plant, nor kill a little spider, simply because it's there. But lets us understand that the web that is spinning is a necessary strand in the great web in which all life is involved" (Frostic, p. 3). Combs and Holland similarly concluded that, "Synchronicity implies a cosmos in which seemingly unrelated events are woven together to form a continuous world fabric" (Combs and Holland, p. 103).

Theories of a noosphere or some "Universal Mind" would be as insubstantial and incredible as any other unprovable speculation if it weren't for the genuine phenomenon of meaningful coincidence. Significant acausality instantly and completely wrenches consideration of an all-pervasive cosmic intelligence from the purely theoretical down to the immediately demonstrable. After satisfying ourselves that such events are not merely irrelevant accidents inevitably encountered over the course of an ordinary lifetime, we can begin with the recognition of synchronicity. When we do this, our rational alternatives suddenly narrow to an inescapable conclusion: that an otherwise unseen consciousness unifying and organizing all matter, energy, and actions in existence compassionately communicates with each individual through personally symbolic events. If so, then we see that coincidences that appear acausal actually find their origins in this superconscious that does not abrogate the laws of nature for the sake of synchronicity but makes it possible through natural laws still unknown to us, since these occurrences often connect human beings with physical, natural phenomena.

Meaningful coincidence continues to preoccupy some of our time's leading thinkers. Alfred North Whitehead, considered by many to be the twentieth century's most influential mathematician, concluded that synchronicity (which he referred to as *Novelty*) was "the secret fractal dimension of reality." Today, popular philosopher Terrence McKenna, using Whitehead's terminology, tells his audiences that "there is a transcendental force at work upon the temporal landscape of the planet."

Accepting the fact of meaningful coincidence makes it possible for us to follow a line of implication that leads toward its ultimate source; after all, a meaningful message implies a sender. Meaning implies purpose. Purpose implies organized intent. Organization implies an organizer with a design plan. A plan implies a planner. A design implies a designer. Whether we refer to this cosmic designer as God, Logos, the Universal Mind, or any of the other assorted labels we feel most comfortable with, it remains a personality force, or conscious will. It is the broadest common denominator in the universe, a purposive intelligence to whom questions of space, time, and relative size are all alike. It organizes the motion of galaxies with the same sense of intent with which it sends synchronicity into the lives of individual human beings.

This is about as far as a rational understanding of the phenomenon can take us. A logical acceptance of meaningful coincidence grants that a cosmic intelligence not only exists but communicates through apparent reality shifts specifically directed toward us as individuals. By way of an entirely reasonable approach to synchronicity, we proceed no further than Cicero was able to reach in 45 B.C. It was then he published his *De natura deorum* (*On the Nature of the Gods*), in which he compared the search for God to that of a man who arrives at a magnificent mansion, goes inside, and finds a splendid feast of wine, meat, and fruits among golden and silver plates and bowls spread out on a great table illuminated by brilliant candles and surrounded by rich cushions. Soft music fills the air, but neither performers nor the host are to be seen. The man goes from room to room, looking in vain for the generous person who has organized such a luxurious banquet.

In other words, God's existence is self-evident in the organized bounty of nature. But anything beyond that is unknown and unknowable (Grant, p. 524). The yearning of Cicero's hypothetical dinner guest for a direct experience of God could not be satisfied, because he undertook a rational search that led him from room to empty room. He assumed that something as material as a banquet presupposed a physical host.

However, as the preceding pages have attempted to demonstrate, human beings have other ways of knowing. God exists, but if His essence cannot be encompassed by reason, it must lie beyond reason. Campbell's definition is as comprehensive as it is accurate: "'God' is a metaphor for a mystery that absolutely transcends all categories of thought." In other words, God's existence is a mystery that dwells within the field of experience. And the human experience that seems to access that mystery is meaningful coincidence. We may learn something about such experiences from the different individuals I studied. They all spoke of an initial awe that thrilled their whole being with a sense of participating in some transcendent mystery far greater than, yet including, themselves. In such moments, time itself becomes irrelevant. It is replaced by a sensation of oneness with some living eternity, accompanied by feelings of compassion. What happens goes on as much inside as around them. They are simultaneously humbled and inspired, moved and awestruck.

While the "meaning" or presumed intention of synchronicity is not always clear or even intelligible, our volunteers reported that the real value of their experience was found in "going with the flow," in allowing themselves to feel the connection with the moment. In doing so, they felt their souls or subconscious had been nourished, whether or not they consciously grasped what had been presented to them. They understood it internally and with something other than the rational mind, which had been outstripped by the spiritual magnitude of the experience. In this expanded vision of reality, their previous conception of the world, in which a strictly limited linear progression of events was unswervingly dominated by observable instances of cause and effect, became as suddenly obsolescent as pre-Copernican notions of the Earth being the center of the universe. Ordinary consciousness fumbled frantically to explain it away, minimize, devalue, control, or, failing all else, discard it. But even a relatively low-energy synchronicity generated in the research members an intuitive certainty of its spiritual authenticity.

Simple, nonjudgmental appreciation, which didn't necessarily mean accepting that the coincidence was anything cosmically significant, was generally sufficient to open up an inner knowing, a primal sureness, however irrational, that the event was meaningful. During synchronicity, even the initially skeptical among our volunteers felt that the hitherto impossible or, at most, doubtful realm of spirituality interfaced with the sphere of material existence. They seemed to be standing in an Otherworldly field of action where time and space intersected to connect with a personal thought in the Universal Mind, the ordering principle that underpins every aspect of nature. They stood for a timeless moment at the focal point of creation itself, not as an accidental fluke of probability, but because there was a mutual transference of high significance. For them, meaningful coincidence was at once an individual experience and a materialization of the organizational will of the universe. The human microcosm and the cosmic macrocosm intersected at a special point in time to become one for an immeasurable instant.

Synchronicity is the long-lost, direct experience with God. If some designing force does indeed reveal its interpenetration of all things through moments of synchronicity, then we may conclude that we personally, as well as every cell in our body, are likewise connected to and part of the Universal Purpose. We err in believing that we and God are separate entities, distinct not only from each other but from the rest of creation. In a synchronous event, God begins to identify Him/Herself as the sum total of every item comprising the whole universe. Each particle of creation is a living detail of the Creator, whose complete identity is expressed only in the totality of existence. If this conclusion is valid, then God is still in the process of creation, as the universe continues to expand outward and, with it, our individual destinies. We are co-creators, the latest attempt (on Earth, at any rate) by the Cosmic Mind to express and understand itself through human consciousness.

Jung discovered when treating his patients that the degree of their psychoses stood in direct relation to their level of such spiritual convictions. Lack of any religious, philosophical, or cosmic views went along with the deepest neuroses. He found, too, that restoring his patients' lost spirituality or giving them one for the first time resulted in a correspondent improvement in their condition. He deduced from these observations that a spiritual instinct was part of the human psyche. To back up his assertion, we can cite the fifteen-thousand-year-old burial caves of the Near East, where Neanderthal men and women sprinkled the corpses of their loved ones with red dust and covered them with garlands of flowers. Faint traces of both the funereal ochre (which apparently signified blood) and flowers (universal archetypes for love and bereavement) were recovered by archaeologists, who believe these discoveries are physical proof that even hominids preceding modern humans had already developed and even ritualized some spiritual belief in the soul and its survival after death.

Jung's corollary has important bearing on synchronicity and its significance for modern people's ongoing spiritual crisis, which, at base, is the failure to experience catharsis in a world of scientific cynicism. Modern science reduces existence to a depersonalized mechanism, while institutionalized religions are more concerned with maintaining their relevance than they are with inspirational power. But the gap between science and spirituality (the material and spiritual spheres, respectively) is bridged by every meaningful coincidence, because it connects our visible, physical existence with an invisible spiritual reality. At once a great scientific and spiritual thinker, Teilhard de Chardin bridged that gap in himself. Another scientist who attempted to synthesize the material and spiritual worlds was Albert Einstein.

Einstein was a true scientist, not because he satisfied the academic requirements expected of him by his teachers and peers, or even because he made important discoveries in modern physics.

His genuineness as a scientist in the classic and highest sense originated in his lifelong willingness to admit that he could be wrong.
Several times in the course of his studies, he found that former
positions which had seemed almost inviolable had to be abandoned
because of valid contradictory evidence. For example, during most of
his life, he refused to accept meaningful coincidence as a credible
correspondence connecting human beings to space and time. But
before his death in 1955, Einstein began to reconsider the subject
and opened himself to its possibilities, as the following quotation
suggests:

> *The most beautiful and most profound emotion we can
> experience is the sensation of the mystical. It is the sower
> of all true science. He to whom this emotion is a stranger,
> who can no longer wonder and stand rapt in awe, is as
> good as dead. To know what is impenetrable to us really
> exists, manifesting itself as the highest wisdom and the
> most radiant beauty which our dull faculties can com-
> prehend only in the most primitive form—this knowledge,
> this feeling is at the center of true religiousness. The
> cosmic religious experience is the strongest and oldest
> mainspring of scientific research. My religion consists of a
> humble admiration of the illimitable superior spirit who
> reveals himself in the slight details we are able to perceive
> with our frail and feeble minds. That deeply emotional
> conviction of the presence of a superior reasoning power,
> which is revealed in the incomprehensible universe, forms
> my idea of God. (MacCracken, p. 58)*

The high utility of meaningful coincidence is its ability to bring
about spiritual catharsis. Synchronicity is catharsis. It represents
genuine spiritual experience in a world where such phenomena are
more than circumspect. If, indeed, as Jung believed, we possess a
spiritual instinct, perhaps many of our problems, in terms of both
individual alienation and social dislocation, are caused by our
current failure to exercise it. Restoring this spiritual instinct could
have the same concurrent rise in the emotional health of our clearly
neurotic society that Jung's psychotic patients experienced when he
administered to their souls as well as to their subconscious. A synchronous event in one's life gives an immediate infusion of spiritual

certainty brought about through individual connection with the Otherworld. Nothing is more convincing than personal experience, especially when it goes deeper than our rational mind to touch the soul in a transpersonal experience.

Some individuals doubt they own a soul because they have never felt its existence. Synchronicity has the power to shake a person into awareness of the soul. It is the golden key, searched for by generations of thinkers, to unlock the reality of spiritual existence. In connecting with such an emotionally transfiguring force, we are again capable of that which the Greeks knew as *katharsis*, a purging of the human soul when encountered by the Divine. Only at such moments are mortals convinced of the verity of their own souls, because they feel them. As Campbell said, "The seat of the soul is where the inner and outer worlds meet" (Campbell, p. 105).

It is precisely this cathartic experience, the missing link with spiritual reality, that we rediscover in meaningful coincidence. It is our individual lifeline to that Compassionate Mystery that speaks its care to us in symbols meant specifically for us. Even beyond the cosmic guidance thus available and the thrilling conviction that we are being personally addressed by the Spirit of Existence itself, we benefit from realizing with our innermost being that we have a right to be here, that we figure significantly and needfully into the enigmatic scheme of an expanding universe, whose ultimate purpose, although still veiled in secrecy, is inseparable from our own destiny.

Synchronicity instills compassion for all living things, because it helps us to see that each one is an important piece in the growing mosaic of Creation, which is an unfinished artwork that would be diminished by the loss of a single fragment. Because we stand so close to it, the totality of the mosaic image escapes us, until meaningful coincidence provides the proper perspective. A deepening appreciation of our meaningful coincidences so attunes our own heartbeat with the external pulse of the cosmos that we experience a sense of being in sync with existence. It is only through such a synchronization of inner and outer worlds that we attain an elusive still-point, where the entire universe seems poised in perfect balance on the fulcrum of our soul. Here is the secret place of tranquillity, the repository of personal peace, the holy of holies. And it is not found on a mountainside or in a church, but in one's own heart. The Cathedral of God lies in every human breast.

Since meaningful coincidence is the method whereby we can attain this ultimate goal of every creed, synchronicity may be thought of as its own religion—as the Everyman Religion—if only because synchronous events happen to every human being. They are our own miracles and revelations that ground us in the certitude of a spiritual dimension, grant us direct experience of the Creator, and guide us in developing a reverence for and comprehension of the creation. Synchronicity is religion without dogma, wherein all are free to draw their own conclusions from personal experience. Each man is his own priest; each woman, her own priestess. The supreme authority from which they obtain unfiltered guidance is neither a pope nor a guru but the Designer of Nature. Appreciation of synchronicity inculcates spiritual self-reliance and engenders philosophical self-esteem. No religion could want for anything more, and few have ever attained so much.

Our visible sphere of physical phenomena stands in relation to the invisible sphere of an organizational force underlying it in the same way a musical sound track bridges the action and keeps the dramatic impetus of a feature film moving along from beginning to end. Absorbed in the story unfolding on the screen, members of the audience are consciously unaware of the score, save when the music swells in a climax. Subconsciously, of course, everyone closely following the motion picture constantly keys into corresponding, universally understood musical symbols that imprint the film's predetermined mood on the emotions of its spectators. So too, the spiritual matrix of our own life story goes largely unseen but is felt subconsciously, except in climactic moments of synchronicity brought about through the manifestation of archetypal symbols. In other words, if spiritual power is the sound track of our existence, its every fortissimo is a meaningful coincidence.

Whether we use the modern metaphor of a film score or the ancient analogy of Indra's net, the ordering power that gives purpose to every detail in the universe is invisible because it is the thought of a Cosmic Mind, with whom each one of us is a co-creator. The ultimate goal of that creation is mysterious. But its secrets are revealed by the compassionate Architect of Existence every time we experience synchronicity.

The chief goal of this book has been to encourage you to take up the challenge of meaningful coincidence. Its classifications aim at providing fixed definitions for this elusive phenomenon by bringing it into clearer focus. And anecdotal examples underscore its reality in human behavior. Most important, however, the methods used for interpreting synchronicity and integrating it into your life can elevate you to new levels of psychological well-being and self-enlightenment. America's outstanding thinker of the mid-nineteenth century, Ralph Waldo Emerson, affirmed that the greatest discoveries are those we make about ourselves. There is no more effective means of making those self-discoveries than embracing the synchronicity that punctuates our earthly existence. Its value derives from the assumption that everything you need or want to know lies within yourself, and that accessing synchronicity will bring you the kind of discoveries Emerson esteemed as the most precious.

Because they are often so deeply personal, understanding the meaningful coincidences that signpost their way through our lives brings us into a truly thrilling accord with the Ultimate Mystery. They are empowering experiences that inspire us to take up the hero's journey in search of our destiny. By applying the simple techniques of interpretation and integration, you will be on your own Grail-quest toward the authentic life. Feelings of meaning and purpose will suffuse your spirit, making you a more confident and competent person. As a woman in our research group who'd had her own share of joy and tragedy told me, "The more I pay attention to synchronicity, the more everything in my life makes sense."

Synchronicity & You is your guidebook to finding the mystical potential in your own life. Use it!

Bibliography

"Andrew recalls 'Eerie' News of Brown's Death." *St. Paul Pioneer Press*, 12 November 1995.

"A Watery Coincidence." *The Chicago Sun-Times*, 20 July 1995.

Bach, Marcus. *The World of Serendipity*. Englewood Cliffs, NJ: Prentice-Hall, 1970.

Bolen, Jean Shinoda, M.D. *The Tao of Psychology, Synchronicity and the Self*. New York: Harper & Row, 1979.

Buxton, Michael. *Juan Crisostomo Arriaga, Orchestral Works*. Madrid, Spain: Academie de San Francisco, 1995.

Campbell, Joseph. *The Masks of God*. New York: Harper & Row, 1988.

Carson, David, and Sams, Jamie. *Medicine Cards: The Discovery of Power Through the Ways of Animals*. Santa Fe, NM: Bear & Co., 1988.

Cirlot, J. E. *A Dictionary of Symbols*. New York: Philosophical Library, 1962.

Combs, Allan, and Holland, Mark. *Synchronicity, Science, Myth and the Trickster*. New York: Marlow & Co., 1989.

Cranston, William. "The Spear of Destiny." *Alternatives Magazine*, vol. 4 (June, 1987).

"England's Oldest Man." *The Chicago Tribune*, 28 March 1997.

Emerson, Ralph Waldo. *The Complete Writings of Ralph Waldo Emerson*, compiled with an introduction by Compton F. Smith. New York: Mansfield Publishing Co., 1897.

Figuerido, C. A., *El arte y la mente del musico J. C. de Arriaga*, Bilbao, Spain: Colombo, 1949.

Frostic, Gwen. *Beyond Time*. Hackensack, NJ: Dolphin Press, 1990.

Goldberg, Bruce. "Synchronicity." *Fate Magazine* (November, 1996).

Grant, Madison. *Great Thinkers of the Ancient World*. New York: Scribners and Sons, 1922.

Grasse, Ray, "Life as Guru: The Synchronistic Teachings of Everyday Life." *Quest*, (Summer, 1996).

Gray, Timothy, and Tanous, Alex. *Dreams, Symbols and Psychic Power*. New York: Bantam Books, 1990.

"Happy Birthday." *Fate Magazine*. (August, 1998).

H.C.R.L. *Encyclopaedia Britannica*. Chicago: Encyclopaedia Britannica, 1976.

Hicks, Jim, series ed. *Mysteries of the Unknown*. Alexandria, VA: Time-Life Books, 1990.

Hillman, James. *Re-Visioning Psychology*. New York: Harper & Row, 1975.

Hindley, Geoffrey, ed. *The Larouse Encyclopedia of Music*. New York: Crescent Books, 1986.

Jacoby, Werner. *The Life of the Buddha*. New York: Riverwoods, 1896.

Jung, Carl Gustav. *Synchronicity*, trans. R.F.C. Hull. New York: Princeton University Press, 1973.

Kazan, Elia. *A Life*. New York: Alfred Knopf, 1988.

Kozminsky, Isidore. *Numbers, Their Meaning and Magic*. New York: Samuel Weiser, 1977 (reprint of 1912 original).

Krassner, Mark. *The Life of Leibniz*. New York: Grosset & Dunlap, 1958.

Kubiczek, August. *Hitler Was My Friend*, trans. H. Roth. New York: Grosset & Dunlap, 1961.

Lake, Medicine Grizzlybear. *Native Healer*. Wheaton, IL: Theosophical Publishing House, 1991.

Leach, Maria, ed. *Funk & Wagnalls Standard Dictionary of Folklore, Mythology and Legend*. New York: Harper & Row, 1972.

MacCracken, Raymond. *The Life and Mind of Albert Einstein*. Chicago: Regnery Publishers, 1978.

McHenry, James. *Ignatius Donnelly*. Saint Paul, MN: Minnesota Historical Society, 1968.

McKenna, Terrence. lecture, February, 1991.

Mercatante, Anthony S. *Who's Who in Egyptian Mythology*. New York: Clarkson N. Potter, 1978.

O'Neill, Terry. "The Hat Came Back." In *Fate, True Reports of the Strange and Unknown*. St. Paul, MN: Llewellyn Publications, 1997.

"Opera Singer Dies on Stage." *The New York Times*, 6 January 1996.

Peat, F. David. *Synchronicity: The Bridge Between Matter and Mind*. New York: Bantam Books, 1978.

Plutarch. *Plutarch's Lives*, trans. C. W. Oldham. London: Atheneum Press, 1950.

Poe, Edgar Allan. "The Mystery of Marie Roget." In *The Complete Works of*

Edgar Allan Poe. New York: Roundtop Press, 1898.

"Premonitions of the Titanic." *Fate Magazine.* (December, 1994).

Reimer, Margaret. *Coincidence.* Toronto: Inner City Books, 1980.

Rig Veda, trans. Richard Strongless. London: Hartsford, 1952.

Ripley's Believe It or Not! 6th series. New York: Doubleday, 1958.

Robertson, Morgan. *The Wreck of the Titan.* Hartford, CT: 7 Cs Press, 1974 (reprint of the 1898 original).

Rodriguez, Jose Antonio Gomez. *Juan Crisostomo Arriaga.* Universidad de Oviedo, Spain (Madrid), translated by Angela Hernandez, New York: Grosset & Dunlap, 1958.

Ryback, David, Ph.D., and Sweitzer, Letitia. *Dreams that Come True.* New York: Ivy Books, 1988.

Schopenhauer, Arthur. "Transcendent Speculation on the Apparent Deliberateness in the Fate of the Individual." In *Parerga and Paralipomena*, trans. R. H. Furgeson. London: Hardiger House Publishers, 1895.

Solarzano, Brian, ed. *Radio Broadcasts of George Bernard Shaw, 1933 to 1947.* London: Bridge & Sons, 1955.

Spengler, Oswald. *The Decline of the West.* London: Havermill, 1949.

Stickney, John. "Coincidence." *The New York Times*, August 1975.

Teilhard de Chardin, Pierre. *The Writings of Teilhard de Chardin*, trans. Maurice Raben. New York: Three Rivers Press, 1975.

Tevas, Dina. "Remarkable Recoveries and Rescues: Are Miracles on the Rise?" *Fate Magazine*, St. Paul, MN: Llewellyn Publications, June, 1997.

"Titanic Tidbits." *Fate Magazine.* (August, 1998).

"Two Lives, a Weird Coincidence." *San Francisco Chronicle.* 22 April 1978.

van der Post, Laurens. *Jung and the Story of Our Time.* New York: Vintage Books, 1977.

Vaughn, Alan. *Incredible Coincidence: The Baffling World of Synchronicity.* New York: Harper & Row, 1979.

Vidal, Gore. *Palimpsest, a Memoir.* New York: Random House, 1995.

von Franz, Marie-Louise. *On Divination and Synchronicity: The Psychology of Meaningful Chance.* Toronto: Inner City Books, 1980.

Weaver, Warren. *Lady Luck: The Theory of Probability.* New York: Anchor Books, 1963.

"Woman Saved by Dream?" *Atlanta Journal-Constitution*, 8 December